THE SLASHER MOVIE BOOK

THE SLASHER MOVIE BOOK

J. A. KERSWELL

CHICAGO
REVIEW
PRESS

An A Cappella Book

Cover and interior design: Paul Wright
Typesetting: Jonathan Hahn

This edition published in the USA in 2012 by Chicago Review Press, Incorporated
First published as *Teenage Wasteland: The Slasher Movie Uncut* in the United Kingdom
by New Holland Publishers (UK) Ltd.

Chicago Review Press, Incorporated
814 North Franklin Street
Chicago, Illinois 60610
ISBN 978-1-55652-010-5
Printed in China
5 4 3 2 1

DEDICATION

First of all, thank you to everyone who good-naturedly watched a slasher movie late on a Saturday night because he or she was asked to. Your humour and patience have not gone unnoticed. Many people's enthusiasm and knowledge have helped make this book what it is – but I simply don't have the space to acknowledge them all, so I hope they'll forgive me. Thanks to my parents for letting me stay up late to watch horror movies – and, if not exactly encouraging my burgeoning love of the genre, at least turning a blind eye to it. Thank you to Aruna, whose idea over a glass of wine was the chrysalis for this book. My eternal gratitude to the people involved in making these films for taking the time to speak to me. Thanks also to Joseph, Erik, Ryhan, Doug, Ross, Gina, Jake, Dobbs, Amanda and all those at The Bodycount Continues forums. And, to Stuart, for suffering through more slasher movies than most people have had hot dinners.

The slasher defined:

'Some stupid killer stalking some big-breasted girl who can't act, who is always running up the stairs when she should be running out the front door.'

CONTENTS

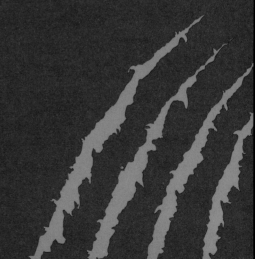

INTRODUCTION

I saw my first bona fide slasher movie at the tender age of 12, back in the early 1980s. *Halloween II* – the 1981 sequel to director John Carpenter's seminal film *Halloween* (the film that launched the Golden Age of slashers) – was the one to pop my cherry courtesy of a clunky Betamax VCR. I was immediately hooked, enthralled by everything about it – the music, the darkness, the unstoppable maniac, the cat-and-mouse action and even the corn-syrup blood.

stores in the United Kingdom carried movies featuring all manner of cannibals, monsters and maniacs. My fun was ultimately spoilt by the moral panic caused by so-called video nasties (see page 126 for more on these), which led many slashers to vanish from UK shelves for years to come.

Even for a self-confessed and unashamed fan like me, it is a little tricky to define the slasher. A

Below Japanese advertisement for *My Bloody Valentine*.

Opposite Iconic artwork for John Carpenter's seminal slasher.

'There's more than one way to lose your heart!'

– My Bloody Valentine

Soon I was searching out more such illicit thrills, but my exuberant drive was thwarted somewhat by my age. The school bus passed by the local cinema, and I would stare longingly at a seemingly never-ending sequence of bloody movies – *Friday the 13th Part 2*, *My Bloody Valentine* and *Happy Birthday to Me* (all 1981). They were tantalizingly out of reach until 1984, when I managed to sneak into *A Nightmare on Elm Street*, but by that time the slasher movie boom was all but over. I had to console myself with feeding my passion on video, and for a few glorious, unregulated years, video

blend of horror and thriller conventions (from earlier films that could be dubbed 'proto-slashers'), it is a cat-and-mouse movie, usually involving a number of teenage victims, at its most basic. The murders are generally outlandish and bloody, invariably

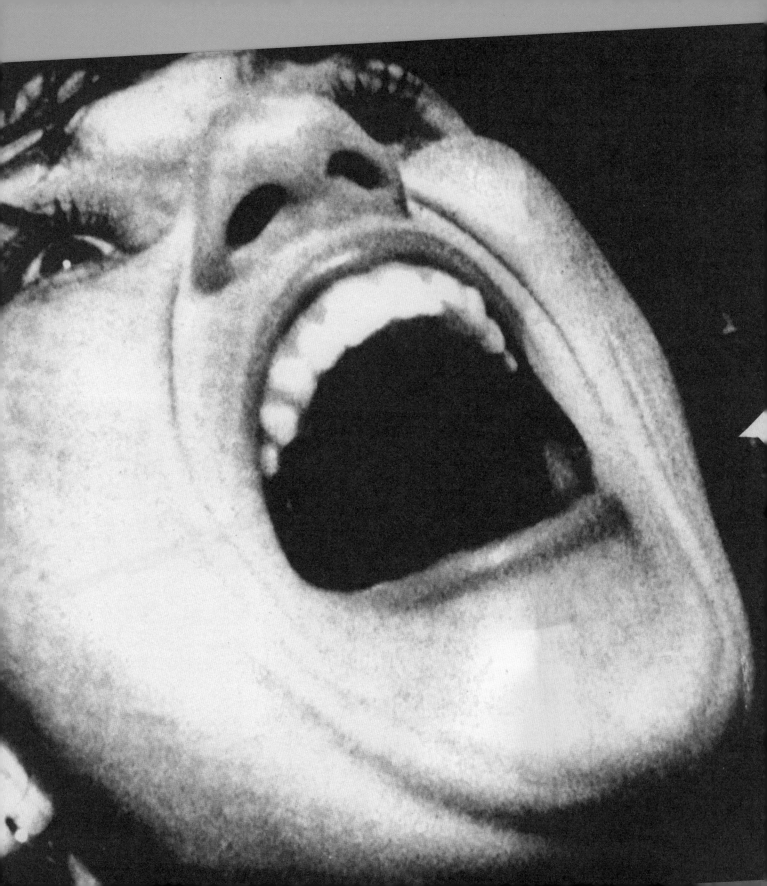

HELL NIGHT ヘルナイト

一作品／アメリカ映画／東宝東和提供
'81年シトヘス恐怖映画祭特別賞受賞

TOWA

シトヘ

字通り不気味な夜に息をひそめ、ついには悲鳴をあげた。最初はアメリカ。次には日本を、そしてあなたを狙っている。

それは、さわやかな夜。学生たちのパーティ

そして現実が恐怖に変わった！

和提供　TOWA

involving the killer brandishing a knife, a machete, an axe or any number of other sharp objects at his victims, for the most part with deadly consequences.

While the location of the slasher movie varies greatly, usually to give the somewhat familiar storyline some individual identity, venues such as fairgrounds, campsites and dorm rooms are generally used as a way of isolating the doomed young cast. The killer is usually driven by a perceived injustice from the past, often related either to the location where most of the action takes place or to one or all of the people in the group.

Left and above
A scream heralds the start of mayhem in Japanese promotional artwork for *Hell Night*.

Right It's the splatter that matters in this Mexican lobby card for *The Prowler*.

The stalker is often (but not always) male, disfigured, masked and also – usually by the last reel at least – quite psychotic. He or she may possess seemingly supernatural powers of regeneration and is likely to be found leaping into frame for one last scare at the film's climax. Increasingly, he or she is hardy enough to show up again in a sequel!

The slasher is a *Boo!* machine, designed to scare and entertain audiences. It appeals to our craving for safe thrills and allows the audience to enjoy the ultimate in schadenfreude while paradoxically cheering on the Final Girl (and *it is* usually a girl) as she fights for survival in the last 30 minutes or so of the movie, after the killer has murdered all of her friends and/or family in a range of increasingly gruesome and inventive ways.

Despite being around in one form or another since the beginning of the movie industry, the slasher is often unfairly seen as bottom-of-the-barrel horror. It is the horror genre's whipping boy, often accused – by critics and genre fans alike – of pandering to the lowest common denominator. Respected genre critic Alan Jones once described the slasher as 'comfort horror', part of its charm being its lethal predictability. But while the slasher movie may rarely challenge, it is horror at its most basic and enjoyable.

Perhaps surprisingly, many slashers from the Golden Age still have the power to unnerve and shock. Watching a one-off theatrical showing of the original *Friday*

JESUS SOTOMAYOR

¡MATA BELLAS MUJERES!
¡DESTROZA A LOS HOMBRES!

EL ASESINO DE ROSEMARY

SI LO ATRAPA... USTED DESEARA LA MUERTE!

¡LA MAS CRUEL Y SANGRIENTA HISTORIA JAMAS FILMADA!

con FARLEY GRANGER y VICKY DAWSON - Director: JOSEPH ZITO

Right The killer does
some teen pruning
in *The Burning*.

Below Japanese
promotional artwork
for *The Burning*.

the 13th (1980) about 10 years ago, the guffaws turned to stunned silence once the axe began to fall. Part of the pleasure of yesterday's horror movies is that many still hold up today and just as many have improved with age, now boasting an air of camp and cheese to add to their already irresistible appeal. For example, *Halloween* (1978) is still a sleek shock machine, despite its bell bottoms and seemingly antiquated teen talk.

The Slasher Movie Book takes an affectionate yet critical overview of the popular history of the slasher. However, writing a book on films that most critics have turned their backs on is fraught with difficulties. Myths and inaccuracies have sprung up around many films, and I have attempted to unravel these mysteries as best I can. For some of the more obscure films, such as *Savage Water* (1978) and *Blood Beat* (1982), almost no information exists. Other films, such as *The Prey* (1980), for example, languished on the shelf before getting a cinematic release or going straight to video, and some made it to neither. The date given for each film is that of the cinema release in the country of origin, unless otherwise stated. Box office figures are always expressed in US dollars, unless otherwise stated.

It would be impossible to cover every movie ever made in this subgenre – especially given the glut of straight-to-DVD slashers still being regularly released. However, *The Slasher Movie Book* takes a long, lingering look at the best – and, yes, I guess the worst – that the subgenre has to offer.

The modern stalk 'n' slash movie as we know it was born when John Carpenter unleashed his bogeyman on small-town America in 1978 with *Halloween*, but the film wasn't created in a vacuum and draws on many earlier genres. *The Slasher Movie Book* traces the roots of the subgenre in folklore and violent French theatre. Violent

ンメントの世界で長らくヒットを世に
サーである。これまでにフランク・シ
エル、バニー・マニロウらのコンサー
ュージカルの脚本も書いており、舞台
「エルヴィス・フォーエバー」、映画は
本にも多大の協力を惜しまなかった。
ラマックス・フィルムの副社長で次回
当している。

特殊効果トム・サビ二
TOM SAVINI

アメリカ全土を呑み込む現在のホラ
ぬきにして語ることは出来ない。
「十三日の金曜日」「ドーン・オフ
アック」「ゾンビ」など、さまざまな
手がけている。観客の恐怖心理をつか
果を生み出す才能は、まさに天才的と
ら絶大な信用を受けている。
特殊効果の他に、メイク・アップ、
も手がけ、最近作「ナイト・ライダー
として活躍している。

監督トニー・メイラム
TONY MAYLAM

英国王立演劇アカデミー出身の秀才
し、ドキュメンタリー・シリーズで早
ている。その中には、ポール・ニュー
バーンらの主演作があり、どちらも大
映画第一作は、インスブルック冬季
の長篇ドキュメンタリー「ホワイト
スクワ映画祭で受賞したのを始め、
数の賞に輝いた。以後、ランク・オ
ケル・ヨーク、ジェニー・アガター主
ブ・ザ・サンズ」を監督した。今回、
にデビューしたが、ハリウッドはま
わけだ。

THE **BURNING**

Pro
use
the
or g
enti
eith

7

The BURNING

©CROPSY VENTURE MCMLXXX

Below Slashers were just as popular on the small screen. American TV ads for *Prom Night*.

Right For the chop: Japanese advertisement for *Friday the 13th Part 2*.

horror thrillers from Europe were hugely instrumental in shaping the subgenre, and I examine the *krimi* (the term used in Germany for crime or mystery thrillers) of the 1950s and 1960s, the stylish and sexy *giallo* (meaning yellow) from Italy in the 1960s and early 1970s, and even the home-grown goings-on in Pete Walker's drolly macabre 1970s British shockers. (The term '*giallo*' originates from the yellow-covered crime and murder fantasy books popular in Italy since the 1920s). Similarly, I discuss how early horror films, including

Alfred Hitchcock's *Psycho* (1960), as well as bloody drive-in features and movies such as *Black Christmas* and *The Texas Chain Saw Massacre* (both 1974), all played their part in the subgenre's evolution.

Illustrated with colourful artwork from all over the world, *The Slasher Movie Book* concentrates on the era that I (and many other fans) consider the Golden Age of the slasher movie – the period from 1978 to 1984. *Halloween*'s success in 1978 opened the floodgates for imitators and gave birth

If You're Not Back By Midnight... You Won't Be Coming Home!

PROM NIGHT

Fear stalks the high school prom! A fiendish killer seeks revenge on four romantic teenagers who share one terrifying secret!

Leslie Nielsen • Jamie Lee Curtis

FIRST TIME ON TV!

9:00PM 2,6

4 TV GUIDE

THE HAPPIEST DAY OF THEIR LIVES BE A NIGHT OF GRADUATING TERROR...

PROM NIGHT

Starring JAMIE LEE CURTIS and LESLIE NIELSEN

Parental Discr

TONIGHT 9PM

to another slasher movie classic – *Friday the 13th*. For six furious (and glorious) years, nowhere in America seemed safe, and high schools and summer camps ran with teenage blood; every holiday was marked with a flash of the knife. *The Slasher Movie Book* revels in this most disreputable of subgenres and also touches on the cultural impact of the genre on society and on other subgenres.

In this book, I also look at how the slasher movie descended into straight-to-video hell, while Hollywood continued to plunder its excesses to spice up mainstream thrillers. Getting into the game relatively late, countries outside America, from India to Mexico, began producing their own versions of the slasher – often with jaw-dropping results. However, its true resurrection came in the mid-1990s with Wes Craven's *Scream*, launching a similar flood of imitations. Today the slasher movie packs multiplexes just like it did 30 years ago. Needless to say, just like most slasher movie villains, this is the subgenre that just won't die.

My love affair with the slasher movie has endured through the very best and the very worst of the subgenre. In hindsight, the promise of the thrill – the tantalizing terrors that the mind of a young teenager could dream up – often left me disappointed, but I have kept on watching slasher after slasher to try to replicate that delicious frisson of terror, the one that I experienced at age 12 when viewing *Halloween II* for the first time.

BLOODY BEGINNINGS – GRAND GUIGNOL TO PSYCHO

From childhood fairy tales and legends to the adult fare of Mary Shelley's *Frankenstein* (1818) and Bram Stoker's *Dracula* (1897), we have always been intrigued by the desire to be frightened, and our fascination with violence has endured.

As with other types of entertainment, it was the moving picture that brought the slasher to the masses. The horror movie proved to be an immediate favourite with the public, and many of the films that came before John Carpenter's seminal film *Halloween* provided a heady brew of influences. These proto-slashers slowly shaped what we now consider to be the slasher movie formula. Few films that were made pre-Hitchcock's *Psycho* could be described as slasher movies per se, but many other genres – literary, theatrical and cinematic – helped mould the subgenre, including a form of theatre found in late 19th-century Paris, Le Théâtre du Grand Guignol.

GRAND GUIGNOL – THE THEATRE OF BLOOD

Today the term 'Grand Guignol' (which literally translates as 'big puppet show') refers to any entertainment that deals with horror – especially the gloating, visual use of extreme graphic violence. Founded by Oscar Méténier in 1897, the theatre originally staged naturalistic plays. Five or six short plays – anything from suspense thrillers to sex farces – were performed nightly and would invariably feature characters from the city's underclasses. The Grand Guignol's main attractions were its horror plays, however.

With titles such as *Le laboratoire des hallucinations* and *L'horrible passion*, these plays often climaxed with staged acts of torture, murder and mayhem, and they presented a particularly bleak world in which villains rarely received punishment. Early gore special effects saw throats slashed, eyes ripped out and faces burned off with acid. Perhaps realizing that this crowd-pleasing horror was the main reason for the theatre's success, playwright André de Lorde (who took over the theatre's directorship in 1898) helped cement the Grand Guignol's notoriety as he put on an increasing number of plays with insanity as their main theme.

The theatre, which flourished for over 60 years, was most popular between the two world wars (1918–39), when it became infamous around the world and also one of Paris's leading tourist attractions. One of its best-known actors, Paula Maxa, who was dubbed the 'most assassinated woman of all time', was allegedly murdered on stage more than 10,000 times in at least 60 different ways and was raped as many as 3,000 times, according to *The New Yorker* magazine (18 March, 1957).

The popularity of the Grand Guignol began to wane after 1945, however, as the audience's desire to be frightened had been all but exhausted by the brutal reality of the gruelling Second World War.

As the curtain began to fall for the last time, cinematic violence in horror films

'These plays often climaxed with staged acts of torture, murder and mayhem.'

began to grow more graphic – Georges Franju's remarkable French horror film *Eyes Without a Face (Les yeux sans visage*, 1960) is a notable example. It depicts an obsessed surgeon who murders young women and removes their faces in order to try to restore his daughter's ruined beauty. The film, which showed gory scenes of surgery in gloating close-up detail, had French audiences reeling. Highly

influential, John Carpenter cites the white mask that the daughter Christiane wears in Franju's film as an inspiration for the faceless look of Michael Myers in *Halloween* some 18 years later.

In 1962 the Grand Guignol closed its doors for the last time. However, its influence was felt long after the physical theatre was demolished. The desire of the Grand Guignol's audience to be scared

Above The Grand Guignol tradition lived on in *Eyes Without a Face*.

COUNTRY OF ORIGIN AND PRODUCTION U.S.A.

"The CAT and the CANARY"

from the comfort of their own seats has
subsequently resonated throughout horror
cinema. It laid the groundwork for the corn
syrup and latex gore extravaganzas of the
early 1980s.

The kind of visceral violence seen at
the Grand Guignol rarely made it onto
cinema screens until the early 1960s, as
seen in such films as the aforementioned
Eyes Without a Face. However, there were
a few early Grand Guignol cinematic
adaptations, the first in 1912 with the
Maurice Tourneur–directed production *The
Lunatics* (*Le système du Docteur Gudron et
du Professor Plume*).

In the United States, an outcry from the
public over perceived immorality in the

'A hidiously deformed maniac, who believes he is a cat, is on the loose.'

movies led to the introduction of the Hays
Code in 1930. It provided a set of industry
guidelines that severely restricted what
could be shown in film, making even
mild references to sexuality and brutality
unacceptable. This arguably prevented the
excesses of the Grand Guignol crossing the
Atlantic (at least at that time). That said,
horror thrillers were still popular on the

American stage, and they really set the ball rolling for the emerging subgenre of the slasher.

FROM THE AMERICAN AND BRITISH STAGES TO THE SCREEN

Perhaps not as well-known as British crime writer Agatha Christie, the American Mary Roberts Rinehart was a major influence on the genre and the development of the new slasher subgenre. *The Bat* (1926) was based on a dramatic adaptation of the Rinehart novel *The Circular Staircase* (1908) by the author and Avery Hopwood. This serio-comic film portrays guests in a remote mansion who are menaced by a thief and killer in a grotesque bat mask. *The Bat* spawned the 'old dark house' film craze and, in turn, the fledgling slasher movie.

After the success of *The Bat*, Universal Studios released the silent masterpiece *The Cat and the Canary* (1927) based on John Willard's 1922 stage play. The film brings a stark expressionism to the tale of relatives gathered together for the reading of a will. The only beneficiary (Laura La Plante) must prove her sanity at the end of the night, but news arrives that an escaped lunatic – a hideously deformed maniac who believes he is a cat – is on the loose. Like *The Bat*, the film is atmospheric and is shot through with tension-relieving humour. The film also has lengthy point-of-view (POV) shots as the camera prowls the dusty mansion; POVs became the mainstay of the slasher. The secret doors behind bookcases might seem a tad creaky by today's standards, but the cat-and-canary analogy continued to ring true over the following decades, as countless victims were subsequently stalked by killers.

The Old Dark House (1932) was another film of this type. Based on a novel by J. B. Priestley, it was directed for Universal Pictures by English director James Whale, probably best remembered for the iconic *Frankenstein* (1931) and *Bride of Frankenstein* (1935). As with *The Cat and the Canary*, the plot finds a group of people in danger; in this case five urbane travellers are caught out by a vicious storm in the wilds of Wales and take refuge at a house inhabited by a strange, eccentric family. The brutal and drunk manservant, Morgan – played to great effect by Boris Karloff – releases a psychotic pyromaniac from the attic with entertaining and of course frightening consequences.

This theme of pitting town dwellers against strange country folk (or vice-versa) is a recurring theme in later slashers. The isolation of a group of people in an alien environment became a staple of the slasher movie. *The Old Dark House* also foreshadows the subgenre by utilizing the idea that the sins of the fathers return to haunt the children years later, providing a catalyst for the violent mayhem. Similarly, a plot featuring a madman let loose and cat-and-mouse chases around the central location, in this case the manor,

Below A maniac is on the prowl in *The Old Dark House.*

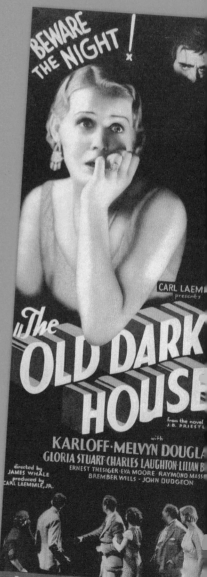

Below A savage killer attacks in the atmospheric *The Leopard Man*.

also became a staple feature in films of the subgenre (see the Golden Age chapter, pages 70–155).

EARLY INFLUENCES

Also released in 1932 was George Archainbaud's *Thirteen Women*, which preempted the later slasher 'body-count' films, starring Irene Dunne and Myrna Loy (who later found fame in *The Thin Man* films). Loy plays a psychotic woman who uses hypnosis and suggestion to kill the former classmates who wouldn't let her join their sorority because of her Japanese-Eurasian heritage. As they die, she crosses through their yearbook photos, a device later borrowed by slashers such as *Prom Night* (1980). The film climaxes with Loy stalking her final victim on a train and meeting a messy end – bringing to mind the closing minutes of *Terror Train* (1980), another film in which an event that occurred at college provides the catalyst for a killer's demented revenge.

Other early examples of maniacs on the prowl include *The Terror* (1928), based on the play by writer Edgar Wallace, whose books would find great popularity

in Germany in the 1950s and 1960s as *krimis* (see pages 38–43). Only the second film ever to use sound, *The Terror* features a homicidal maniac who dresses in a cloak and hangman's hood and lurks below an inn. The villain's bizarre attire nods towards the masked maniacs that stalked our screens during the subgenre's Golden Age more than 50 years later.

Boris Karloff returned to the old dark house genre in his first British movie, *The*

Women Alone the Victims of Strange, Savage Killer!

THE LEOPARD MAN

with DENNIS O'KEEFE · MARGO

Ghoul (1933), in which he returns from the dead to seek revenge on his heirs gathered together for the reading of his will. *Night of Terror* (1933) features horror legend Bela Lugosi (most famous for his role as Dracula) and an ending in which the killer returns from the dead, foreshadowing the cliché of the killer coming back to life for one last scare that was so prevalent in the slashers of the 1970s and 1980s.

Also drawing on the creature theme seen in *The Bat* and *The Cat and the Canary*, director Jacques Tourneur and producer Val Lewton's atmospheric *The Leopard Man* (1943) features a series of savage murders in a small town committed by either an escaped leopard or a killer on the loose. Tourneur keeps the audience guessing with the same masterful air of unease and suggestion that made his *Cat People* (1942) so remarkable.

The Basil Rathbone shtick *The Scarlet Claw* (1944) was one of a series of successful Sherlock Holmes films. Revolving around murders committed with a garden weeder – the scarlet claw of the title – the film features shots of the killer raising the murder weapon above his head and bringing it down repeatedly, an action

that would later become commonplace in the subgenre. The killer at one point dresses as a woman, foreshadowing the transvestism in *Psycho* (1960) and in De Palma's *Dressed to Kill* (1980).

Particularly influential on the development of slasher cinema was the work of Agatha Christie. The 1939 book *Ten Little Indians* is probably one of Christie's best-known works, certainly one that has been adapted for theatre, film and television many times, with its first screen adaptation, *And Then There Were None*, in 1945. By gathering a group of people – who have each committed a crime but have so far escaped detection – in an isolated setting and bumping them off one by one,

Above Even Sherlock Holmes was on the trail of a proto-slasher in *The Scarlet Claw*.

Below StereoVision 3D murder in *House of Wax*.

Christie unwittingly provided the blueprint for slasher plots, even to this day. Each of the murders in Christie's novel parallels a verse in a nursery rhyme (on which the book's title in based), after which one of ten toy soldiers is removed. This seemingly perverse merging of objects of childhood innocence with murder became especially popular in slasher cinema – perhaps most significantly in the 1970s *giallo* thrillers of the highly influential Italian director Dario Argento (see pages 52–53).

What is especially interesting about Christie's book, though, is how she simplifies the rules of the thriller to allow for as many murders as possible. Again, this has parallels with the later slasher movie, where the thriller elements are often secondary to the visual representation of the murder – and this reaches its logical conclusion in movies such as *Friday the 13th*, in which the bodycount is the main attraction.

Another influential film was Robert Siodmak's atmospheric *The Spiral Staircase* (1945) based on Ethel White's novel *Some Must Watch*. Set in 1916 in a small American town, it finds a serial killer murdering women with physical disabilities. An old woman (Ethel Barrymore, great-aunt of Drew Barrymore who starred in *Scream*) fears that her young mute maid (Dorothy McGuire) might be next on the killer's list. The use of a seemingly helpless but sympathetic young

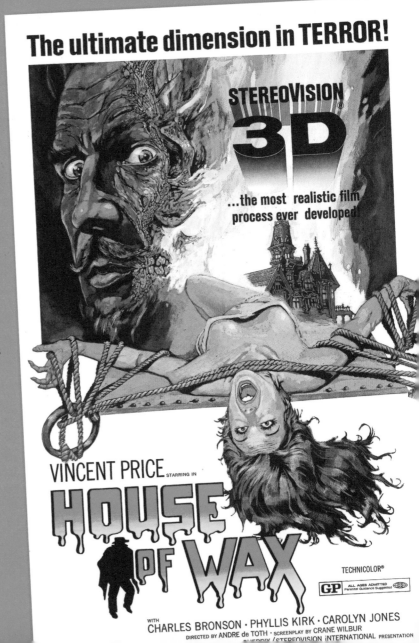

The ultimate dimension in TERROR!

STEREOVISION 3D

...the most realistic film process ever developed!

VINCENT PRICE STARRING IN

HOUSE OF WAX

TECHNICOLOR®

GP ALL AGES ADMITTED Parental Guidance Suggested

WITH CHARLES BRONSON · PHYLLIS KIRK · CAROLYN JONES
DIRECTED BY ANDRE de TOTH · SCREENPLAY BY CRANE WILBUR
STEREOVISION iNTERNATIONAL PRESENTATION

woman who then goes on to become the heroine is something that would become commonplace in later slasher films, as the Final Girl is the last person left standing. *The Spiral Staircase* is also interesting in preempting the subgenre visually, with shots of the killer lingering behind a tree in a thunder storm or watching his next victim from the depths of a closet. It also features false scares, a killer in black leather gloves, the killer's POV, and an 'Oh, it's you!' moment. Most would become so overused in subsequent slasher films that they became clichés.

Originally released in 3D, *House of Wax* (1953) sees a sculptor (Vincent Price) take revenge on the people who he blames for destroying his wax museum and leaving him hideously burnt. This period piece saw Price decked out in what would become the de rigueur *giallo* outfit of black leather gloves and hat. The sustained suspense scene, when a young woman is chased through foggy streets by the 'phantom' – flapping like a black raven in his cape – was played out again and again in many subsequent slasher movies.

Based on a novel by Fredric Brown, the 1958 *Screaming Mimi* provocatively promised 'suspense around every curve'

Below Knife play in *Jack the Ripper*.

¿Por qué Fueron Siempre sus Víctimas Mujeres de la Noche?

El balancear de una bolsa...
El vaivén de las caderas...
Un cuerpo sensual...
El repentino vibrar de un cuchillo... y después... un sofocado ruido de pasos escapando...
¡EL REPETIRIA SU BRUTAL ACTO DE MATAR UNA Y MIL VECES MAS!

JOSEPH E. LEVINE presenta

EL DESTRIPADOR DE LONDRES

Opposite The slasher movie hits a watershed moment with Alfred Hitchcock's highly influential *Psycho*.

'Screaming Mimi provocatively promised suspense around every curve.'

on its posters. It delivered – at least in the curve department – with Federico Fellini's muse, the voluptuous blonde Anita Ekberg, playing an exotic dancer. In a remarkable opening sequence, Ekberg is attacked while taking a beach-side shower by a psychopath who has just escaped from an asylum and holds a knife dripping with blood. It anticipated the famous shower scene in *Psycho*, in which another blonde (Janet Leigh) is menaced in remarkably similar circumstances.

The loose British dramatization of the infamous Victorian Whitechapel murders, *Jack the Ripper* (1959) was slapped with an X rating on its UK release. Many slasher films take elements of real-life cases and spin fiction out of them, but few are straight adaptations of actual murders. The main exception to this is the Whitechapel case, which has been adapted numerous times. Here Jack attacks young women, with a fetishistic emphasis on the knife that he pulls from his medicine bag. A jazz soundtrack by Stanley Black accompanies the action, which reaches a hysterical crescendo during the murder sequences. Jack's hulking silhouette, sustained terror

A new kind of drama and excitement from the screen's master of suspense...
as his cameras move into the icy blackness of the unexplored!

FRED COCK'S

YCHO

CERT 'X'

starring
ANTHONY
PERKINS

VERA
MILES

JOHN
GAVIN

co-starring
MARTIN
BALSAM

JOHN
McINTIRE

and
JANET
LEIGH
as
MARION
CRANE

Directed by
ALFRED
HITCHCOCK

Screenplay by
JOSEPH
STEFANO

A **PARAMOUNT**
Release

PRINTED BY LEONARD RIPLEY & CO., LTD., LONDON, S.E.11

one... BUT NO ONE... will be admitted to the theatre after the start of each performance of PSYCHO.

Above Janet Leigh (as the ill-fated Marion Crane) screams during the film's iconic shower sequence.

Above right Italian poster for *Psycho*.

scenes and POV camera work foreshadow many slasher films.

Another British film – also released in 1959 – anticipating the slasher cycle is Terry Bishop's *Cover Girl Killer*, set around the seedy world of strip clubs and tawdry glamour photo shoots of London's backstreets (a similar setting to the following year's controversial *Peeping Tom*). It features a master-of-disguise, moralizing killer who stalks models. It is interesting that – like a good number of subgenre films – it takes a dim view of sex and violence while at the same time exploiting them for maximum effect.

PEEPING TOM

The seminal British film *Peeping Tom* (1960) was released in the United Kingdom a month before Hitchcock's *Psycho* hit American screens. It was incredibly controversial when first released, and the negative critical reaction all but ended director Michael Powell's career. *Peeping Tom* still retains the power to shock some 50 years later.

A young man (Carl Boehm) has been left traumatized by the studies into fear that his father forced him to participate in when he was a child. Now grown up, he has taken up a horrific pastime: killing women and filming their dying throes. A young neighbour (Anna Massey) might prove to be his redemption or his next victim.

Ahead of its time, *Peeping Tom* is not a 'safe' horror film: it allows us to see through the eyes of the killer – effectively also questioning the audience's role as the voyeurs of violence. Boehm – as with Anthony Perkins in *Psycho* – is an attractive young man, not the hideous monster killer of many earlier (and, indeed, later) films – and this new concept would have confused audiences. Powell was ahead of his time in many ways; perhaps 1960 audiences were also not ready to see a film dealing with themes of child abuse and sadomasochism.

HITCHCOCK'S *PSYCHO*

Released in 1960, *Psycho* was Hitchcock's 49th picture and one that very nearly didn't happen. The director, stinging from the commercial and critical failure of *Vertigo* (1958), noticed that low-budget horror thrillers were making money at the box office. Accordingly, Hitchcock bought the rights to the 1959 novel *Psycho* by writer Robert Bloch. The events in the book – and in turn, the film – were loosely inspired by the real-life murders by Ed Gein in Wisconsin in the 1950s (which involved transvestism, necrophilia and cannibalism and Gein dressing in dead women's skin). Although Bloch and Hitchcock without a doubt stretched the boundaries of what was acceptable with audiences at the time, only the quasi transvestism and the murders were utilized in *Psycho*. Unfortunately, equating tranvestism with mental illness in *Psycho* serves to date the film.

Later Gein-inspired films such as *The

Below And this is why she's screaming: Anthony Perkins (as Norman Bates) dons his dead mother's attire.

Below American poster art for William Castle's *Homicidal*. The first – but certainly not the last – would-be Hitchcock beater.

Texas Chain Saw Massacre and *Silence of the Lambs* (1991) were much more explicit in their portrayal of cannibalism and bodily mutilation, but these themes were clearly beyond the pale for audiences, and even Hitchcock, in 1960.

SPECIAL "FRIGHT BREAK"

here will be a special FRIGHT BREAK uring the showing of "Homicidal." All hose too timid to take the climax will e welcomed to the COWARD'S CORNER!

THE STORY OF A PSYCHOTIC KILLER !

HOMICIDAL

WILLIAM CASTLE PRODUCER

GLENN CORBETT · PATRICIA BRESLIN · EUGENIE LEONTOVICH · ALAN BUNCE · JAMES WESTERFIELD · AND INTRODUCING JEAN ARLESS

Written by ROBB WHITE · Produced and Directed by WILLIAM CASTLE · A WILLIAM CASTLE PRODUCTION · A COLUMBIA PICTURES RELEASE

'She might have fooled me but she didn't fool my mother.'

– Norman Bates, *Psycho*

When Hitchcock first pitched *Psycho* to Paramount, the studio hated it and refused to let the director make it on its back lot. Characteristically, Hitchcock remained unconcerned. The director had flirted with the dark and macabre in earlier films such as *Jamaica Inn* (1939) and *Rebecca* (1940). He had also produced an early take on the Whitechapel murders in *The Lodger* (1927). *Psycho* – which enabled Hitchcock to continue his apparent obsession with victimizing his leading (usually blonde) ladies on-screen – was a few shades darker than was expected even of Hitchcock, although it was always his intention to inject humour into the film.

In Bloch's novel, the character of Norman Bates was unattractive and in his 40s. Instead Hitchcock hired established star Anthony Perkins, a geeky but handsome 28-year-old actor, to play Bates. Janet Leigh was hired as the ill-fated Marion Crane, the woman who finds herself at a near-deserted motel run by Norman Bates, who appears to be henpecked by his invalid mother. After accepting dinner, Marion retires to her room for a shower. It is here that she is

COLUMBIA PICTURES presents **HOMICIDAL** starring GLENN CORBETT, PATRICIA BRESLIN, EUGENIE LEONTOVICH, ALAN BUNCE, JAMES WESTERFIELD and introducing JEAN ARLESS. A WILLIAM CASTLE PRODUCTION

suddenly attacked by what looks like an old woman stabbing at her savagely with a butcher's knife. In a twist, it turns out that Norman's mother is dead and the young man has gone mad after years of abuse and now shares his fractured mind with his overbearing mother. Every time he is attracted to a woman, the 'mother side' of his mind turns homicidal.

Psycho pushed the envelope on what was acceptable in screen violence, sexuality and even bathroom apparatus (it was the first time a toilet had been seen flushing in a Hollywood film). The film's shower

murder is, of course, one of the most iconic – and imitated – scenes in the history of cinema. Its ability to shock today has been lessened by overfamiliarity, but it is still remarkable. The unnerving score by Bernard Herrmann is integral to why the scene works so well. Surprisingly, Hitchcock originally intended it to play without music, but the film would have undoubtedly lost much of its power to frighten without it. The strings stab like the frenetic movement of the knife on-screen. The discordant, high-pitched repetition of one note in quick succession jars the

Above Jean Arless goes psycho in *Homicidal*.

COLUMBIA PICTURES presenta a

STRASBERG
RONALD **LEWIS**
ANN **TODD**
en

BAJO NINGUNA CONDICION PODRA EL PERSONAL DE ESTE TEATRO REVELAR AL PUBLICO EL INCREIBLE FINAL DE ESTA PELICULA!

"UN GRITO DE TERROR"
·SCREAM OF FEAR·
co-estrella CHRISTOPHER **LEE**

Escrita y Producida por **JIMMY SANGSTER** Dirigida por **SETH HOLT** UNA PRODUCCION HAMMER FILM

Above Mexican lobby card for Hammer's *Taste of Fear*.

audience and makes it immediately aware that something horrible is going to happen. It is probably one of the most influential pieces of music in horror-movie history.

Anthony Perkins's performance as Norman Bates is also remarkable. One minute he's charming and bashful, the next he's bubbling with resentment – his madness appears and then vanishes like the sun behind fast-moving clouds.

None of the people involved with

Psycho's production were especially known for horror films – Hitchcock included – which heightened the impact on audiences previously used to his polished and debonair thrillers. The shower murder and the killing of the detective Milton Arbogast on the landing quite literally sent audiences into hysterics. Similarly, Hitchcock's decision to kill off the protagonist Marion a short time into the film threw audiences off-kilter. They must have expected Janet Leigh's blonde and slightly clueless Marion Crane to be the heroine in the film, not its first victim. Marion's death, both titillating (a naked blonde in the shower) and extremely violent, became the prototype for subsequent slasher victims. Perhaps ironically, Leigh's real-life daughter, Jamie Lee Curtis, became the archetypal survivor and Final Girl in *Halloween* almost 20 years later. Similarly, in a nod to the legacy of *Psycho*, Wes Craven used the same gimmick of killing off the most recognizable cast member first – a blonde Drew Barrymore – in his postmodernist slasher *Scream*.

The influence of *Psycho* on the development of the slasher movie cannot be underestimated. *Psycho* was the culmination of a lurid melting pot of thriller and horror conventions. The movie was inspired by low-budget horror and thriller films, and it launched a veritable tidal wave of imitators and knock-offs.

One of the first was by William Castle. Best remembered for his gimmick-laden horror films, such as *House on Haunted Hill* and *The Tingler* (both 1959), Castle

made his would-be *Psycho*-beater *Homicidal* in 1961. He upped the ante by showing the blood gush during a frenzied knife attack. *Homicidal* also takes *Psycho*'s quasi transvestism and makes it central to the plot. Like many of Castle's films, it is deliciously camp. *Homicidal*'s gimmick was the 'fright break', a 45-second timer before the film's climax as the heroine–cum–Final Girl approaches the house where the killer lurks.

Perhaps surprisingly, the bulk of the post-*Psycho* thrillers were not American-made films. Closely following *Homicidal* was *Taste of Fear* (1961), the first of the *Psycho*-inspired cycle from the British studio Hammer. It was followed by *Maniac* and *Paranoiac* (both 1962), *Nightmare* (1963), *Fanatic* (1964), *The Nanny* (1965) and the Freddie Francis–directed minor

Below More typically ghoulish Mexican lobby-card artwork for *Psychopath*.

British thriller *Hysteria* (1965). Hammer's cycle finished with *Crescendo* (1969). Rival British studio Amicus also got in on the act with the Bloch-scripted *Psychopath* (1965).

Back in America, Richard Hilliard's *Violent Midnight* (1963) introduced many of the elements that would become ubiquitous in the subgenre in later years, including a voyeuristic POV shot of the killer pulling down a branch to get a look at a potential victim. Knife murders ensue near a women's college by someone in army boots, black gloves and a fedora hat. The shots of the killer's boots stalking prey are eerily similar to those used in the Golden Age slasher *The Prowler* (1981).

Below Gore galore in *Blood Feast*.

Another scene, in which a drunk amorous couple go skinny dipping at midnight in a lake and are attacked, would be right at home in any *Friday the 13th* movie.

Crown International's *Terrified* (1963) has a striking opening five minutes, with a laughing, masked lunatic pouring cement into an open grave as a teenage boy screams for help. This cheap production has many shots of people wandering around an abandoned ghost town to little effect but is, at least, notable for having a killer in a mask (a balaclava) – a contrast to the fresh-faced monsters that followed Norman Bates. Alongside *Violent Midnight*, *Terrified* may have been among the first of the teen slashers – but it certainly wouldn't be the last.

In 1963, nine years before he made *The Godfather*, Francis Ford Coppola directed *Dementia 13* for producer Roger 'King of the Bs' Corman. Made on a shoestring – reputedly for less than $45,000 – it is a grisly tale of axe murders at an Irish castle, where a group gathers to commemorate the death of a family member. Coppola joined the band of directors who progressed to bigger, if not always better, things, including *Terror Train*'s Roger Spottiswoode (who made the 1997 Bond movie *Tomorrow Never Dies*) and *The Final Terror* (1983) director Andrew Davis (who went on to make the 1993 Harrison Ford thriller *The Fugitive*).

The year 1963 also saw what is widely credited as the first 'gore' film, *Blood Feast*. Director Herschell Gordon Lewis was

¡Un clásico drama de terror! Hiela los huesos." —REVISTA LIFE

El sensacional astro de "Tom Jones" aparece ahora como un desequilibrado asesino

Above Mexican lobby card for *Night Must Fall*.

the first to really exploit the successes of the Grand Guignol, at least in terms of viscera and explicit violence, for a drive-in audience. It was the splatter that mattered in this badly acted, suspense-free, tongue-in-cheek effort. Hated by critics, the gore proved to be a big hit with audiences. Lewis admitted that the storyline of a killer targeting women to use their body parts to bring a dormant Egyptian goddess back to life was not much good, but the film was the first of its kind. Lewis continued with a string of gory shockers, including *Two Thousand Maniacs!* (1964), *Color Me Blood Red* (1965) and *The Gruesome Twosome* (1967). Lewis's low-budget gore epics paved the way for the explicit hyperviolence of *Friday the 13th* and *Maniac* (1980).

The success of *Psycho* attracted Hollywood talent to the genre. Making much of its axe murders was William Castle's *Strait-Jacket* (also 1964) with Joan Crawford, who decapitates her husband and lover in the opening moments. The one-time queen of Hollywood went on to star as the ringmaster in the murder-at-the-circus opus *Berserk* (1967).

Right Deliciously lurid Belgian artwork for *The Haunted House of Horror*.

Far right American poster for *The House That Screamed*.

'1950s teen icon Frankie Avalon . . . gets stabbed in the crotch with a scimitar.'

In 1964, MGM released *Night Must Fall* – a British remake of its 1937 film. Albert Finney plays a psychopathic axe murderer who keeps a severed head in a hatbox. The 1960s closed with more British gore with the surprisingly violent *Corruption* (1967), starring the usually mild-mannered Peter Cushing as a mad killer.

The first British splatter movie, *Twisted Nerve* (1968), attracted considerable negative attention for seeming to equate psychosis with Down syndrome. Lewis J. Forces's deliciously ironic *Night After Night After Night* (1969) had the killer turn out to be a crazed judge. From the British studio Tigon, *Haunted House of Horror* (1969) almost fitted the latter Golden Age slasher formula perfectly, with a group of hedonistic teens partying in a deserted gothic mansion, only to be carved up by a lunatic whose behaviour is triggered by a full moon. If you ever wanted to see the 1950s teen icon Frankie Avalon – here at least 10 years too old for the part – get stabbed in the crotch with a scimitar, then this is definitely the film for you!

Andy Milligan's low-budget American film *The Ghastly Ones* (1969) lived up to its

name with disembowelling by pitch fork and axe. In Spain, *The House That Screamed* (1969) was a stylish variation on *Psycho*, featuring violent slasher murders that thematically preempted later films such as *Pieces* (1982).

Meanwhile, while *Psycho* was shocking audiences in America and Britain, the Germans were carving themselves a slice of the action, producing violent films that spiced up the English thriller with *Psycho*-esque levels of violence.

THE GERMAN *KRIMI* – EDGAR WALLACE SPEAKING

It would be impossible to talk about the slasher without referring to the other European subgenres that influenced it, including the German *krimi* (which simply translates as crime or mystery thriller).

Krimis were the originally hugely popular German adaptations of the crime novels of British writer Edgar Wallace, probably best remembered now as the cocreator of *King Kong* (1932). His books were often peppered with garish murders, invariably set around Scotland Yard or in smog-filled London or the English countryside. Highly prolific, Wallace wrote around 175 novels, which have been popular in Germany since the 1920s when the first film adaptations of his books appeared.

Below A hooded claw attacks in *Creature with the Blue Hand* (1970).

In film, the *krimi* was at its height of popularity from the end of the 1950s to the mid-1960s (although it was still being made into the early 1970s). Mostly filmed in Germany, the *krimi* films fetishized England and presented a decidedly Germanic idea of Englishness, which produced an almost otherworldly, alternative reality. They were often scored with jazz – both urgent and incidental – by composers such as Martin Böttcher and Peter Thomas. This helped update old stories, giving them a contemporary edge. These *krimis* are typically peopled by dastardly villains in outlandish costumes – featuring everything from a green skeleton in a cape to a whip-grasping monk in a red habit and pointy hat.

Increasingly flirting with the horror genre, the *krimi* satisfied the conventions of the crime caper as well as Teutonic farce. A good number of English-dubbed versions were released in the American market – although pruned of nudity and other distinctive features – and most ended up on TV with the horror elements pushed to the foreground.

The Wallace *krimi* to launch the craze was 1959's *Fellowship of the Frog* (*Der Frosch mit der Maske*). It has the eponymous villain terrorizing London, alternating heists with murder. The frog – in a mask with ludicrously bulging glass eyes – would not be out of place in a *Scooby Doo*

Der NEUESTE
Edgar Wallace Krimi
Der Mönch mit der Peitsche

Above From out of the fireplace emerges a flamboyantly attired villain in *The College Girl Murders* (1967).

Left Fellowship of the Frog started the *krimi* craze.

Below Klaus Kinski was perhaps the only actor to appear regularly in *krimis* as well as *gialli* and American slashers.

'The murderous goings—on are fueled by greed and criminality.'

Die blaue Hand

cartoon. The film features brief flashes of bloody violence (a British policeman has his throat slit with a straight razor) and an increasingly tongue-in-cheek approach, which helped point the way forward for the genre. Phenomenally successful, it launched a whole slew of similar adaptations and imitations – including *The Green Archer* (*Der grüne Bogenschütze*, 1961) and *Dead Eyes of London* (*Die toten Augen von London*, also 1961). The Rialto studio produced 32 *krimis* alone.

Wallace's son, Bryan Edgar Wallace, took over the reins from his late father. *The Strangler of Blackmoor Castle* (*Der Würger von Schloß Blackmoor*, 1963) is based on his novel and portrays a stalker in a black balaclava and leather gloves prowling the grounds of a British castle. The killer carves an 'M' onto the heads of his victims before decapitating some of them. Anticipating the elaborate death scene as the showstopper in subsequent slasher films, one poor individual loses his head while riding a motorcycle. As with most *krimis*, the murderous goings-on are fuelled by greed and criminality.

Structured even more like a slasher movie (with a vicious murder every 15 minutes or so) is *The Phantom of Soho* (*Das Phantom von Soho*, 1964), with many POV shots showing a large knife held by sparkly, golden-gloved hands. It closes with an effective stalking sequence in the luggage section of an airport, before the de rigueur unmasking of the killer.

In *Room 13* (*Zimmer 13*, 1964), savage

Above and right
Bloodshed and nudity
in *Room 13* was a
winning formula that
provided a blueprint
for later slashers, as
indicated by these
images taken from
the Edgar Wallace–
inspired film.

Edgar Wallace
Zimmer 13

Right Monkey business in this Mexican lobby card for *Gorilla Gang*.

'The Italians quickly became the masters of the knife – upping the levels of violence.'

razor killings rock the genteel 'English' countryside. Especially given that it's vintage, there are a couple of jolting moments, including the murder of a stripper. Not only does she briefly flash her nipples, but her airborne arterial spray is also far more graphic than you might expect in a film from this time.

Perhaps because of sheer saturation and repetition, the *krimi* began to lose its appeal by the late 1960s. *Gorilla Gang* (*Der Gorilla von Soho*, 1968), according to film historian Kim Newman, was the series' jump-the-shark moment. Even for films where disbelief must always be suspended – and the colourful nature of its villains taken for granted – a lumbering maniac in a gorilla suit is impossible to take seriously.

Several of the latter entries were coproduced in Italy and were sold as *gialli* there and *krimis* in Germany. However, the Italians quickly became the masters of the knife, as their violent slasher thrillers – which had evolved alongside the *krimi* – upped the levels of violence, sleaze and sheer artistry to become a cultural and box-office phenomena all of their own.

Una historia fantástica que pudo ser verdad... Una leyenda que duró doscientos años...

USTED GRITARA ATERRORIZADO

DISTRIBUIDA POR

DEATH STALKS ON HIGH HEELS – THE ITALIAN *GIALLO*

The *giallo* takes its name from a series of lurid thrillers with trademark yellow covers (*giallo* means 'yellow' in Italian), which first appeared in Italy in 1929. Typically Latin in nature, the *giallo* took the staid crime novel and spiced it up with doses of sex, glamour and violence – and great soundtracks.

Below Sex, death and madness feature regularly in the *giallo*, as in this typically delirious still from *Death Walks at Midnight*.

Unlike American slasher movies of the 1970s and 1980s, the protagonists of the *gialli* were rarely teenagers. Rather, these films were populated with young, successful 20- or 30-somethings, who sported the latest fashions, thought nothing of jetting off to exotic destinations and were partial to a tipple of J&B Scotch Whiskey (if you thought product placement was a new thing, think again). Mostly eschewing the zany outfits of the *krimi* villains, the *giallo* retained money or madness as the primary driving force for murder.

However, the joys of many *gialli* are the outlandish and often highly improbable plot twists. The *giallo*, which increasingly mixed the horror and thriller genres to great effect, also differed from the later slasher movies by placing much emphasis on detective work to uncover the identity of the killer – either by the police or the protagonists themselves.

THE *GIALLO* TAKES OFF

However, it wasn't until the 1960s that the *giallo* made the transition from page to screen. Despite a few earlier attempts, it is Mario Bava's *The Girl Who Knew Too Much* (*La ragazza che sapeva troppo,*

LA GARRA SANGRIENTA *Dirigido por* LUCIANO ERCOLI TECHNICOLOR

1963) that is widely credited as the first film in the genre. The basic plot follows a serial killer on the loose in Rome and a young tourist (Letícia Román) who may possibly have seen the killer commit the latest murder. Tame by the standards of the excesses of the 1970s, the film features many key elements that would become synonymous with the *giallo*, including a protagonist-turned-detective, a killer on the loose and an obsession with travel and a jet-setting lifestyle.

Bava was reportedly not satisfied with *The Girl Who Knew Too Much*, but his next film, *Blood and Black Lace* (*Sei donne per l'assassino*, 1964), proved to be even more influential to the genre. Highly stylized, the film focuses on a string of murders of models at a fashion house. It introduced the notion of the black-gloved killer armed with a knife, stalking victims and killing them in over-the-top set pieces. The mystery element was strengthened by the use of a mask to hide the identity of the killer. A blank of white instead of a face created a bogeyman, who, in reality, could be any one of the shifty-looking suspects.

'The *giallo* increasingly mixed the horror and thriller genres to great effect.'

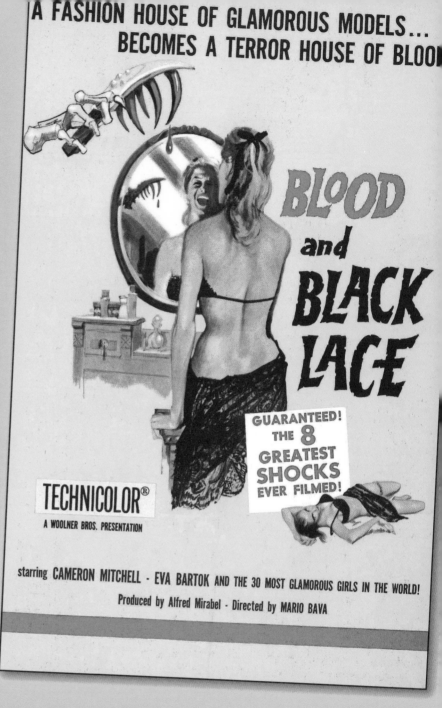

A FASHION HOUSE OF GLAMOROUS MODELS...
BECOMES A TERROR HOUSE OF BLOOD

BLOOD and BLACK LACE

GUARANTEED! THE 8 GREATEST SHOCKS EVER FILMED!

TECHNICOLOR®
A WOOLNER BROS. PRESENTATION

starring CAMERON MITCHELL · EVA BARTOK AND THE 30 MOST GLAMOROUS GIRLS IN THE WORLD!
Produced by Alfred Mirabel · Directed by MARIO BAVA

Above American artwork for Mario Bava's seminal *Blood and Black Lace*.

JACK HEDLEY · ALMANTA KELLER · HOWARD ROSS · ANDREW PAINTER
NDRA DELLI COLLI e con la partecipazione di **PAOLO MALCO** Regia di **LUCIO FULCI**
Prodotto dalla **FULVIA FILM** s.r.l.-ROMA Colore LV di LUCIANO VITTORI

Above Italian artwork
for Lucio Fulci's
controversial *The
New York Ripper*.

The blank look invited the audience to
project its own fears onto it – much in the
same way that John Carpenter did later
with 'the Shape' in the great slasher classic
Halloween (1978).

Soon the *giallo* began to gain popularity
with audiences. It also attracted the
attention of directors such as Lucio Fulci
– most famous for his later films such
as *Zombie Flesh Eaters* (*Zombi 2*, 1979) –
who contributed *gialli* such as *Perversion
Story* (*Una sull'altra*, 1969) and the
antiestablishment *Don't Torture a Duckling*
(*Non si sevizia un paperino*, 1972). Umberto
Lenzi made a string of *gialli* beginning with
Paranoia (*Orgasmo*, 1969) and *So Sweet
. . . So Perverse* (*Così dolce . . . così perversa*,
1969), as well as *Seven Blood-Stained
Orchids* (*Sette orchidee macchiate di rosso*,
1972), which was a *giallo-krimi* hybrid
based on a story by Edgar Wallace. Lenzi's
giallo swansong was the wonderfully
trashy *Eyeball* (*Gatti rossi in un labirinto di
vetro*, 1975), which sees a group of tourists
bumped off by a killer dressed in a red
raincoat. The latter device was probably
influenced by the red-coated dwarf killer
in Nicolas Roeg's atmospheric Anglo-Italian
horror-*giallo* hybrid, *Don't Look Now* (*A
Venezia . . . un dicembre rosso shocking*,
1973).

GIALLI IN THE 1970S

The release of two influential *gialli* in 1970
saw Italian cinema awash with black-
gloved killers for much of the early 1970s.
Dario Argento's *The Bird with the Crystal*

Below Lurid Mexican lobby card for *Seven Blood-Stained Orchids*.

47

DEATH STALKS

SIETE ORQUIDEAS MANCHADAS DE SANGRE

LOS CRIMENES MAS PERVE
E INCREIBLES COMET
DIABOLICAMENTE PO
ENFERMO MEN

ELL - PIER PAOLO CAPPONI - ROSSELLA FALK   Director UMBERTO LENZI

EASTMANCOLOR - TECHNOCHROME

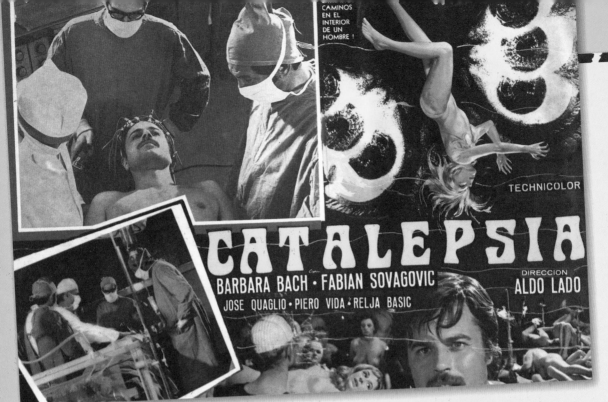

MURDER MUSIC BY MORRICONE

Despite the carnage in the *giallo*, many were blessed with strikingly good soundtracks by composers who went on to become famous. Although perhaps best known for his spaghetti western film scores, Ennio Morricone has scored more *gialli* than any other composer. Morricone's music for the *giallo* has been much imitated – both at the time and since then – but is, in my opinion, rarely made better by other composers. His music reflects the extravagant lifestyles of the cast on-screen (lounge and Brazilian bossa nova beats often accentuated with dreamy, nonsensical female vocals), but he adds in the necessary thriller and horror elements of the *giallo* (discordant meditations on fear and tension).

Morricone's career started in the late 1950s, but in 1970 he composed his first *giallo* soundtrack for Dario Argento's début *giallo*, *The Bird with the Crystal Plumage*. He also scored Argento's *The Cat o' Nine Tails* (*Il gatto a nove code*, 1971) and *Four Flies on Grey Velvet* (*4 mosche di velluto grigio*, 1971), the other film that completed what became known as Argento's 'animal trilogy'. In the 1970s, Morricone contributed memorable soundtracks to many *gialli*, including *Forbidden Photos of a Lady Above Suspicion* (*Le foto proibite di una signora per bene*, 1970), *Short Night of the Glass Dolls* (*La corta notte delle bambole di vetro*, 1971) and *Who Saw Her Die?* (*Chi l'ha vista morire?*, 1972). So popular did his music become that his name was often featured prominently on the film's promotional literature.

EDWIGE FENECH
NOS ENSEÑA ....CUAL ES
EL EXTRAÑO VICIO
de la SEÑORA WARDH

VER SANGRE LE CAUSA UN EFECTO SEXUAL
MEZCLA DE PLACER Y REPULSIÓN ....

Far left Mexican lobby card for *Short Night of the Glass Dolls*, featuring a musical score by Morricone.

Left Giallo queen Edwige Fenech in *Next!*

Below What have They Done to Your Daughters? was released in the United States in 1980 with a new title and artwork to capitalize on the slasher-movie craze.

Plumage (*L'uccello dalle piume di cristallo*), for which Ennio Morricone famously wrote the score (see box opposite), crystallized the disparate elements of the genre to create perhaps the archetypal *giallo* (see feature on Argento, pages 52–53).

The title of Sergio Martino's *Next! (Lo strano vizio della Signora Wardh)* seemed to be a rallying call for *giallo* filmmakers – and it was a call that was certainly answered. *Next!* was the first pairing of the undisputed king and queen of the *giallo*: Edwige Fenech and George Hilton. Fenech plays the wife of an American diplomat, who dodges a cut-throat razor and also a harpoon gun. Hilton is the suave playboy who may or may not be involved in the murders. The suspenseful scene in the underground parking lot where Fenech is menaced by the razor-wielding killer has been copied in many films since,

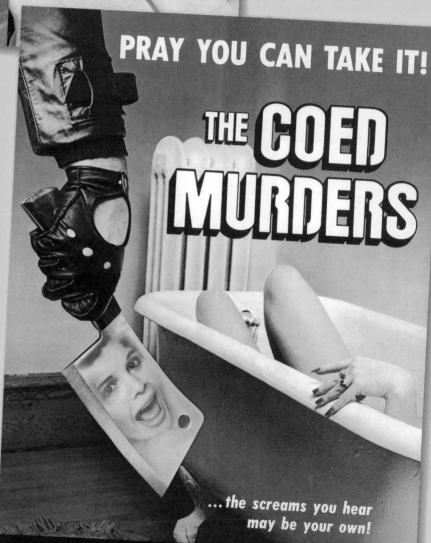

PRAY YOU CAN TAKE IT!

THE COED MURDERS

...the screams you hear may be your own!

Distribuidora ROZIL, presenta a:

GEORGE HILTON · ANITA STRINDB

LA COLA DEL ESCORPION

EVELYN STEWART · LUIGI PISTI

dirección de
SERGIO MARTINI
Color TECHNOCHROME

including Massimo Dallamano's *What Have They Done to Your Daughters?* (*La polizia chiede aiuto*, 1974), as well the early 1980s slasher *Happy Birthday to Me*.

Martino followed with a number of other *gialli*, but *Torso* (*I corpi presentano tracce di violenza carnale*, 1973) appears to have been particularly influential on the American slasher movie. It features a masked killer (often shown through a POV shot) who stalks victims through woods and preys on teenage lovers in a car. There is the theme of a past crime – in this case the death of a child – for which retribution is the motive for the killing in the present. Like teenagers in American slasher movies of the 1970s and 1980s, they smoke dope, enjoy premarital sex and taunt authority. There is the singling out of a Final Girl (Suzy Kendall), whose best protection is that the killer believes she is 'pure'. She discovers all her friends murdered and, in the film's most striking scene, is forced to watch them being dismembered or risk discovery by the killer.

Also very influential on the American subgenre was Mario Bava's darkly comic *A Bay of Blood* (*Reazione a catena*, 1971). The lakeside tale of murder was especially explicit – at odds with his previous *giallo*, *Five Dolls for an August Moon* (*5 bambole per la luna d'agosto*, 1970), in which hardly any blood was spilled. Among the mayhem, a face is whacked with a machete, and a young couple is impaled on a spear as they make love. Unsurprisingly, anyone who has seen *Friday the 13th Part 2* will be aware of a scene almost identical to the

'Among the mayhem, a face is whacked with a machete, and a young couple is impaled on a spear as they make love.'

Far left A Mexican lobby card for Sergio Martino's *The Case of the Scorpion's Tail.*

Below Gialli found a popular and controversial new home on video in the early 1980s. Early British video cover for *Torso.*

TORSO

A FAST MOVING MULTI-MURDER PICTURE ...... GORE & GAL. NOT FOR THE SQUEAMISH ...... VARIETY

THE DARKNESS OF DARIO ARGENTO

Argento is arguably the crown prince of the *giallo*, his films renowned for their visual extravagance and violent set pieces as well as for putting a macabre twist on childhood themes. John Carpenter is said to be an admirer of Argento's work.

Argento once controversially stated he would rather watch a beautiful woman being murdered on film than an ugly one or a man. He is also infamous for including scenes where his real-life daughters and ex-wife, who act in his films, are repeatedly killed off or violently abused for the camera.

The son of movie producer Salvatore Argento, he started his career as a film critic before moving behind the camera to direct the highly influential *The Bird with the Crystal Plumage*

in 1970 (see image above and artwork bottom right). Taking the lead from the *gialli* of Mario Bava, Argento quickly established his trademark elements of beautifully staged set pieces, fetishizing graphic violence, and clever misdirection. The film was a major hit in Italy and grabbed the attention of audiences abroad. Argento followed this with two further *gialli* in what became known as his 'animal trilogy' – *The Cat o' Nine Tails* (*Il gatto a nove code*, 1971) and *Four Flies on Grey Velvet* (*4 mosche di velluto grigio*, 1971). *Deep Red* followed in 1975 (see image top right) and is considered by critics to be one of the best examples of the *giallo* – Argento also considers it his favourite among his own films.

The visually stunning *Suspiria* (1977) kept elements of the *giallo* but was his first foray into the supernatural. Argento didn't return to the genre until *Tenebrae* (1982) and was perhaps inspired to do so by the success of the American slasher movies in the early 1980s. The film's violent set pieces (including an axe to the head and a balletic arterial spray from a severed arm) earned it the dubious honour of being classified as a 'video nasty' in the United Kingdom. Many critics of Argento's movies feel that the quality of his work began to decline afterwards. *Phenomena* (1985) and *Opera* (1987) both attempted to repeat the success of *Suspiria*.

By the 1990s, the smart-set audiences, who had once seen Argento as cutting edge, had long deserted him. In 1993's *Trauma,* in which he directed his own daughter, he unsuccessfully attempted to make a US-set *giallo*. The hallucinatory and visually arresting *The Stendhal Syndrome* (*La sindrome di Stendhal*, 1996) followed. Argento went back to his roots with *Sleepless* (2001), which returned to the obsessions of his earliest films and was regarded as a crowd-pleasing *giallo* by many fans. The 2004 *The Card Player* (*Il cartaio*) was the polar opposite; despite being another *giallo* it eschewed Argento's normal visual extravagances and was met with indifference by audiences. The 2005 TV movie *Do You Like Hitchcock?* (*Ti piace Hitchcock?*) was a homage of sorts to the director of *Psycho* and was similarly overlooked by audiences. The simply titled *Giallo* (2009) received mixed reviews. The director continues to attempt to recapture his early 1970s glory years – and time will tell if he will manage it.

They came seeking pleasure, they found death

Blood Bath

VIDEO MOVIES™ from Hokushin

Above Mario Bava's *A Bay of Blood* got an early video release in Britain with the title *Blood Bath*.

Right American artwork for *The Slasher . . . Is the Sex Maniac*.

American cinemas and drive-ins and helped contribute to the fertile melting pot that gave birth to *Halloween* and the slashers of the early 1980s. There were also Spanish and Turkish films that could loosely be termed *gialli* – they were certainly trying to imitate them – including a number of Paul Naschy films, such as *A Dragonfly for Each Corpse* (*Una libélula para cada muerto*, 1974).

Many *gialli* were released to British cinemas – albeit often promoting sex and nudity above their thriller aspects. The British thriller *Assault* (1971) shares many traits of the subgenre.

Perhaps it is not such a stretch to suggest that Hitchcock himself, the great master of suspense, may have been influenced by the tidal wave of violent thrillers from Italy when he directed his penultimate film, *Frenzy* (1972).

By the mid-1970s, the *giallo* had all but fallen out of fashion, however. *Giallo* budgets and production values plummeted, and some even tried to spice things up by employing hard-core pornographic elements (*Play Motel*, 1979) or overemphasizing the horror and sleaze (*Giallo a Venezia*, 1979) to win back their once-loyal audiences.

The sure death knell for the genre came when spoofs – such as *Death Steps in the Dark* (*Passi di morte perduti nel buio*, 1977) – began to make an appearance. The genre has subsequently failed to repeat the huge mainstream success of its heyday of the early 1970s.

latter. The lakeside setting and the body count approach to the picture led many to assume that the makers of the first two parts of that popular series had been more than a little inspired by Bava's film.

The cross-pollination of the subgenre continued. Many *gialli* were played at

but **THIS IS AS FAR AS WE DARE TAKE YOU...**

with any hope of bringing you back!

FARLEY GRANGER
SYLVA KOSCINA
in

Only beautiful women...
only if they are evil...
and when they are
caught in the act...
he commits the
ULTIMATE BRUTALITY!

the SLASHER

...*is THE SEX MANIAC!*

co-starring SUSAN SCOTT • CHRIS...

DARK DAYS – AMERICAN AND BRITISH GOTHIC (1970–77)

While the slasher cinema of the early 1970s was dominated by the Italian *giallo*, in Britain and the United States the subgenre also continued to develop into what would eventually emerge as John Carpenter's seminal *Halloween*.

Below Mexican lobby card for *And Soon the Darkness*.

The more sensational aspects of Alfred Hitchcock's *Psycho* segued into movies that exploited sex and violence to the hilt. In America many of these films played in the grindhouse theatres (which specialized in exploitation films and cheap B movies) or were shown at drive-ins. Creaky plot devices were largely jettisoned, and madness was celebrated for madness' sake, with the result that the killer was often given the most cursory of motives for his or her actions. Teenagers increasingly moved on from the seats of the cinema, where they formed the core audience, to the screen itself to become the victims of assassins with axes (among other things) to grind.

The period just before the Golden Age of the slasher began with director Robert Fuest's *And Soon the Darkness* (1970). This British psycho-thriller has two young nurses (Pamela Franklin and Michele Dotrice) taking a cycling holiday in France, only to be stalked by a mysterious killer. It moves away from the gothic feel of some earlier examples of the subgenre by unravelling the sinister action in the blistering light of French daytime.

The British thriller *Fright* (1971) finds Susan George foreshadowing Jamie Lee Curtis's predicament in *Halloween*. Menaced by the psychotic father of the child for whom she's babysitting, George spends much of the film being tormented and humiliated, much like in her role in

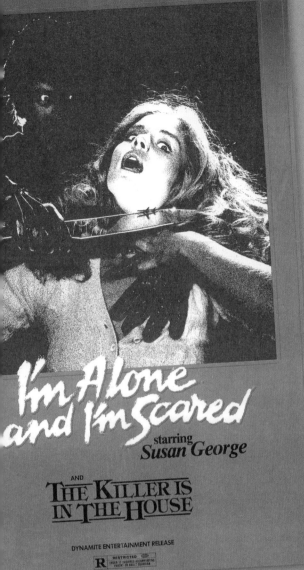

I'm Alone and I'm Scared

starring **Susan George**

AND

THE KILLER IS IN THE HOUSE

DYNAMITE ENTERTAINMENT RELEASE

R RESTRICTED
UNDER 17 REQUIRES ACCOMPANYING
PARENT OR ADULT GUARDIAN

'Frighteningly well made . . . a moral obscenity!'

– Daily Telegraph

foreshadowed Golden Age slashers, telling of a group of young actors stalked by a crazed Shakespearian thespian in a dilapidated theatre at the end of a pier. Unfortunately, by trying to satisfy both the sex and gore crowds, Walker ended up pleasing neither.

Walker's best proto-slasher came next with *Frightmare* (1974), starring the remarkable Sheila Keith as a seemingly benign elderly woman with a terrible secret – she likes to kill people with power tools and eat their flesh! *Frightmare* is a delicious exercise in nihilism and breaks many taboos of the time. On its release its film posters positively screamed the bad reviews, including 'Frighteningly well made . . . a moral obscenity!' from the *Daily Telegraph* – in an effort to draw in the crowds. Courting controversy was obviously Walker's

the better-known cult movie of the same year, *Straw Dogs* – itself an influence on locals-versus-townies films such as *The Texas Chain Saw Massacre* (1974).

PETE WALKER

Perhaps the most influential maker of British proto-slashers was director Pete Walker. *The Flesh and Blood Show* (1972)

Left I'm Alone and I'm Scared was an early 1980s American re-release of the British proto-slasher *Fright*.

Below Power-tool frenzy in this Spanish artwork for *Frightmare*.

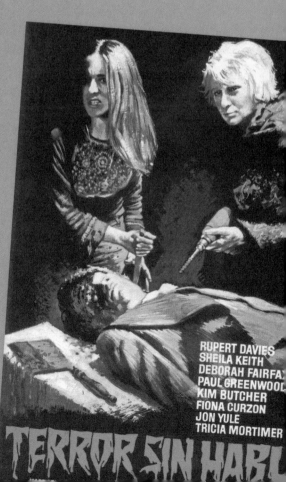

RUPERT DAVIES
SHEILA KEITH
DEBORAH FAIRFAX
PAUL GREENWOOD
KIM BUTCHER
FIONA CURZON
JON YULE
TRICIA MORTIMER

TERROR SIN HAB

Above and centre
Typically outlandish artworks for Pete Walker's *House of Mortal Sin* and *Schizo*.

aim: he believed the bigger the headlines were, the bigger the box office might be.

Again courting controversy, he tackled Catholicism next in *House of Mortal Sin* (1976) in which a young girl visiting confession triggers off obsessional behaviour in a priest, who kills people with objects of worship. In *Schizo* (also 1976),

Lynne Frederick plays a young woman who thinks she's being stalked, and sure enough, bodies start hitting the floor all around her. His last slasher movie, *The Comeback* (1978), seemed positively old-fashioned compared to the same year's *Halloween* but was enlivened by the sweet yet sinister presence of Sheila Keith and a killer in a hag mask.

A NOD AND A WINK: THE BEST AND THE WORST OF PROTO-SLASHERS

It is easy to see why the American *Blood and Lace* (1971) – not to be confused with Mario Bava's rather better-known *giallo Blood and Black Lace* – was dubbed

izofrenia
(SCHIZO)

ESTRELLAS LYNNE FREDERICK · JOHN LEYTON · STEPHANIE BEACHAM
PETE WALKER · Guión de DAVID McGILLIVRAY
Producido y Dirigido por
DE WARNER BROS. (W) UNA WARNER COMMUNICATIONS COMPANY

the killer creeping through the house with a claw hammer, which is very similar to the first appearance of Michael Myers in John Carpenter's much-later film.

The British *Tower of Evil* (1972) features the kind of teenagers who would populate almost all slashers in the next decade. The tagline accurately promised 'They came, they saw, they died!' – as young archaeologists are murdered by a killer at a remote island lighthouse. Robin Askwith,

Below Far-out American artwork for *Blood and Lace*.

the 'sickest PG-rated movie ever made'. The film is set at an orphanage where escapees end up dead but back in their beds so that the evil owner – played by fading Hollywood star Gloria Grahame – can keep collecting money for them. An entertaining mix of unintentional humour and high camp, it has a teenage catfight, a few lashings of gore and a bucketful of sleaze – not to mention a crispy-faced villain, a full 13 years before Freddy Krueger first made an appearance in *A Nightmare on Elm Street*. It also has an opening sequence bearing a remarkable resemblance to the famous opening scene of *Halloween*, with the roving POV shot of

SHOCK AFTER SHOCK AFTER SHOCK as Desire drives a bargain with DEATH!

BLOOD AND LACE

Below left Murder and mayhem in *Tower of Evil* (*Horror on Snape Island*).

Below right Artwork for *Home for the Holidays*.

Far right, top and bottom There's somebody on the phone in the influential *Black Christmas*.

better known for his 1970s sex-comedy work, is impaled with a spear. The film also features copious amounts of nudity.

William Girdler's low-rent *Three on a Meathook* (1972) is a very loose remake of *Psycho* – well, if you can accept the Marion Crane character being played by four teenagers in hot pants and cha-cha heels. The girls meet suitably grisly ends. Like *Psycho*, it was inspired by the real-life crimes of Ed Gein – which were more richly mined later in *Deranged* and *The Texas Chain Saw Massacre* (both 1974).

Released in 1972, *Home for the Holidays* is remarkable in its likeness to later slashers – even more so given that it is a TV movie. A family reunion at Christmas turns deadly when someone in a yellow raincoat starts to ruin Yuletide with a pitchfork. Also released the same year was Amicus's British anthology, *Tales from the Crypt*. In the *And All Through the House* segment, actor Joan Collins kills her husband on Christmas Eve and cannot call the police when an escaped psychopath dressed as Santa is intent on killing her. *Silent Night, Bloody Night* (1973) is an effective low-budget film also with Christmas connections, where a series of murders happen around the site of an old asylum. It seems to have been a large influence on perhaps the best pre-*Halloween* slasher film of the 1970s.

Director Bob Clark's *Black Christmas* (1974) borrows the earlier film's device of creepy phone calls (later utilized to great effect in 1979's *When a Stranger Calls* and *Scream*). His story of sorority girls – including Margot Kidder and Olivia Hussey – being menaced just before the Christmas holidays is a masterpiece of tension, suspense and horror. For once, the

is film is filled with...

SHOCK after SHOCK after SHOCK

HORROR WILL HOLD YOU HELPLESS

HORROR ON SNAPE ISLAND

BRYANT HALIDAY · JILL HAWORTH and introducing GARY HAMILTON as BROM

Executive Producer   Produced by   Directed by   Screenplay by   Based on an original story by GEORGE BAXT
JOE SOLOMON · RICHARD GORDON · JIM O'CONNOLLY · JIM O'CONNOLLY Production for release by THE FANFARE CORPORATION
METROCOLOR   A GRENADIER FILMS, LTD.

There's nothing more chilling than a warm family gathering.

tagline – 'If this picture doesn't make your skin crawl . . . it's on too tight!' – isn't just for show. Both visually and thematically, it is very much a precursor to *Halloween*; it features young women being terrorized by a killer in previously safe environments during an iconic holiday season. It also contains a lengthy scene, shot through the killer's eyes, of him climbing into the sorority house. However, unlike the silent threat of Michael Myers in *Halloween*, the killer here displays a much more orthodox insanity – that of the raving lunatic.

On its release, Clark's film was unfairly criticized as being clichéd by the American film paper *Variety*, which complained that it was a 'bloody, senseless kill-for-kicks feature' that exploited unnecessary violence. It was a modest hit on its release. However, its reputation and importance within the history of the subgenre continued to grow in the years after its release, and today the film remains genuinely frightening.

'If this picture doesn't make your skin crawl . . . it's on too tight!'

Not a slasher as such, the cult sci-fi thriller *Westworld* (1973) features a theme park in which lifelike robots satisfy every fantasy and desire. As with many slashers,

Black Christmas

暗闇にベルが鳴る

'A theme park where lifelike robots satisfy every fantasy . . .'

in which characters do not expect their lives to be rudely interrupted by violence, things do go badly wrong in *Westworld*, and the robots turn on the guests. John Carpenter credited the virtually unstoppable homicidal humanoid – played by Yul Brynner, whose lifelike mask, once

removed, is a faceless void of wires and circuitry – as an influence on his own seemingly invincible masked bogeyman in *Halloween*.

Scream Bloody Murder (1973) bellowed that it was the first motion picture to be dubbed 'gore-nography'. It features a disturbed young man who is sent to an asylum after running over his father with a combine harvester and mangling his own arm. After being fitted with a hook instead of an arm by kindly nuns, he absconds and starts a murderous rampage. It is not a great film, but there are a few odd flashes of visual inspiration and almost poetic

Far left The merciless killer robot in *Westworld* was an inspiration for John Carpenter's *Halloween*.

Below Mexican lobby card for *Scream Bloody Murder*.

Below Double trouble in Brian De Palma's *Sisters.*

Far right Sex and horror combine in *The Single Girls.*

AMESE TWINS AT BIRTH

What the Devil hath joined together let no man cut asunder!

"The most genuinely frightening film since Hitchcock's 'Psycho!'"
— HOLLYWOOD REPORTER

Sisters

ressman Williams presents **MARGOT KIDDER · JENNIFER SALT** in **'SISTERS'**
o-Starring **CHARLES DURNING · BILL FINLEY · LISLE WILSON**
roduced by **Edward R. Pressman** · Directed by **Brian De Palma** · Written by **Brian De Palma** and **Louisa Rose**
Music Composed and Conducted by Bernard Herrmann · Color by MOVIELAB · An American International Release

resonance for future slashers, including one lingering image of blood running down the killer's face like tears.

Brian De Palma has often been accused of imitating Hitchock. His psycho-thriller *Sisters* (1973), released in the same year as the hugely successful *The Exorcist*, is less of a nod and more of a head bang towards the great master's films. Margot Kidder plays two characters who were formerly Siamese twins – one psychotic, the other sweet. De Palma acknowledges his influences from the start, even using Bernard Herrmann – who scored *Psycho* – to provide the music. *Sisters* is full of what can be seen as Hitchcock clichés, but De Palma manages to put a spin on them by using split screens to represent split personalities, for example. He attempts to outdo the shower scene in *Psycho*, something that he almost pulls off.

At the other end of the spectrum is the little-known *Have a Nice Weekend* (1974), a low-budget yawner about a family reunion rocked by murders and endless sandwich making. *The Single Girls* (1974), on the other hand, is significant, as it seems to be spoofing the slasher subgenre four years before *Halloween* supposedly invented it. This semicomic effort is full of wobbly POV shots and murders with garden tools and features a killer who bumps off young women and middle-aged men at an island retreat. "I'm the Girl He Wants to Kill" (1974) was one episode in Brian Clemens's *Thriller*, a women-in-peril British TV show that was tense and suspenseful

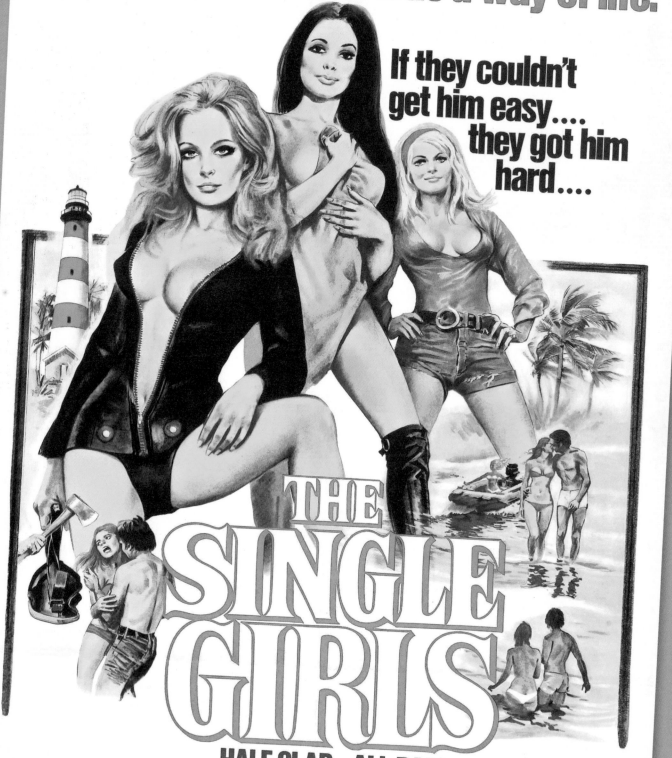

Searching for a man was a way of life.

If they couldn't get him easy....
they got him hard....

THE SINGLE GIRLS

HALF CLAD — ALL BAD!

a Production of SEBASTIAN FILMS LIMITED INC. presents "THE SINGLE GIRLS" starring Claudia Jennings
Jean Marie Engels · Cheri Howell · Joan Prather · Gary...

and featured a secretary being chased around an office by a serial killer.

THE TEXAS CHAIN SAW MASSACRE AND BEYOND

Tobe Hooper's rabid and truly modern low-budget classic *The Texas Chain Saw Massacre* (1974) overshadowed *Black Christmas*. Like many of the best examples of the genre, it concerns a violent clash of cultures and ideals, here the death of late 1960s hippy idealism and the darkly comedic – but terrifying – family of inbred cannibals. The film works on many levels of fear – not least that of being chased by a squealing overweight man who is masked by skin culled from previous victims and waving a chain saw, intent on cutting and consuming his pound of flesh. Norman Bates notwithstanding, Leatherface – the film's main villain – was the first bona fide iconic proto-slasher bogeyman. Despite its fearsome reputation, the film does not show much in the way of visceral violence.

The Love Butcher (1975) was a powder-keg exploitation mix that could only have come about in the mid-1970s, a time when, just before the punk movement broke, boundaries were being tested and

political correctness was, for the most part, unthinkable. In the film, an ugly gardener has a handsome alter ego who punishes the housewives who have previously spurned him. At its heart, a black comedy with dubious sexual politics, the film anticipates later slashers, as the killer, who would be at home in any number of later films in the subgenre, finds lethal uses for household objects and has a confrontation with a Final Girl.

RENÉ CHATEAU présente

APRÈS 5 ANS D'INTERDICTION

STRICTEMENT INTERDIT AUX MOINS DE 18 ANS

MASSACRE A LA TRONÇONNEUSE

UN FILM DE TOBE HOOPER
VERSION INTÉGRALE

A creepy and interesting precursor to films such as *Slaughter High* (1986), the 1976 *Class Reunion Massacre* is marred by a large streak of misplaced misanthropy. A school reunion turns bloody after ex-students are stalked and offed by a killer who dresses in different costumes. They are seemingly targeted because of their supposed 'sins' – including lesbianism.

Around this time, the use of masks comes to the forefront in proto-slashers. In *Savage Weekend*, several couples are stalked by a ghoulishly masked murderer

'That's the last goddam hitchhiker I ever pick up.'

– Jerry, *The Texas Chain Saw Massacre*

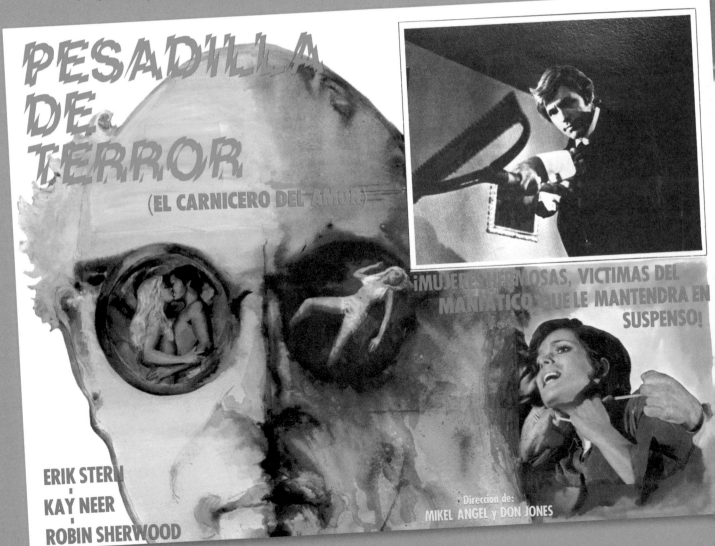

PESADILLA DE TERROR
(EL CARNICERO DEL AMOR)

¡MUJERES HERMOSAS, VICTIMAS DEL MANIATICO QUE LE MANTENDRA EN SUSPENSO!

ERIK STERN
KAY NEER
ROBIN SHERWOOD

Direccion de:
MIKEL ANGEL y DON JONES

Above American video art for *Another Son of Sam*.

Far right American poster art for *The Town That Dreaded Sundown*.

lovelorn teenagers with a burlap sack over his head – the disguise seemingly borrowed by the makers of *Friday the 13th Part 2*. Marred by jarring lurches into comedy, there is, however, a striking murder using a trombone as a deadly weapon!

A killer runs rampant at a college campus in the largely inept *Another Son of Sam* (1977). It was titled to cash in on the real-life Son of Sam murders, which were the work of deranged serial killer David Berkowitz, who terrorized New York City at the time. Despite an evidently low budget, some of the scenes nicely evoke the suburban streets of John Carpenter's soon-to-be-released *Halloween*. The film also includes plenty of POV shots, such as the old hand-comes-into-view-and-pulls-down-a-branch shot.

Wes Craven took another stab at the subgenre after his 1972 attempt, *The Last House on the Left*, when he pitched a middle-class family against cannibalistic desert mutants in *The Hills Have Eyes* (1977). Like *The Texas Chain Saw Massacre* before it, the terror was partially generated by the fish-out-of-water suburban victims menaced by those outside civilization.

However, in 1978 it was John Carpenter and producer Debra Hill who really shook things up when they brought real horror directly into the heart of middle-class suburban America with *Halloween*. The modern slasher movie, as we know it today, was born with that iconic film, and the Golden Age of slashers, which lasted six glorious and gory years, also began.

during a trip to the country. Although it does remarkably anticipate elements in many later films, such as the masked fiends in *Halloween* and the *Friday the 13th* franchises, it is an awkward mixture of sex and thriller elements. Made in 1976, it isn't hard to see why this film sat on the shelf until 1981, when it was released to try to cash in on the slasher boom.

Somewhat better is the evocatively titled *The Town That Dreaded Sundown* (1976), a rare example of a period slasher. Set in Texas in the 1940s, it is based on the real-life, unsolved murders of five people. In the film, the killer is depicted stalking

THE GOLDEN AGE OF THE SLASHER (1978–84)

It was disco death on the terror train that dripped blood on prom night. Teenagers flocked to watch replicas of themselves die in ever-more creative ways, as the pop-culture phenomenon continued to explode onto screens across the world.

The Golden Age of the slasher began in 1978, the year that the horror landscape changed forever with *Halloween*. John Carpenter's film was not released in America until just before the Halloween of 1978, and it was not released in most international territories until 1979. Its success, and that of *Friday the 13th* a few years later, launched a veritable slew of wannabes, rip-offs and riffs on the same theme. The period until 1984 is considered the greatest for the slasher film by many fans. Certainly it is a prolific period in the subgenre, during which over 100 slashers were released. Some were undeniable dross, but there are many gems that are still highly regarded today, among them *Happy Birthday to Me*, *My Bloody Valentine* and *The House on Sorority Row* (1983), all of which I will discuss in the pages that follow.

During this six-year period, the allure of the slasher, for particularly wily producers and directors, was to be able to make significant amounts of money at the box office with a relatively small outlay – and usually without the added cost of bankable stars. As a total, the subgenre made hundreds of millions of dollars at the American box office (see "Bloodbath at the Box Office" on page 202 for a breakdown), and most glided easily into profit.

When those grosses are adjusted to today's rates, they are even more impressive: *Halloween* would have made $144,213,675 and *Friday the 13th* $121,982,066. Even a film such as *When a Stranger Calls* would have raked in an impressive box-office earning of $57,637,681.

Most of these slashers were *Halloween* imitators but lacked the finesse of Carpenter's movie. Taking the deceptively simple template of teens stalked by a murderous figure, the writers and directors put their own spin on it – with varying degrees of success. As a simple rule of thumb, to bring in audiences, you have to give them more 'bang for their buck'. In

'Bit by bit . . . by bit he carved a nightmare!'

– The Toolbox Murders

other words, subsequent slasher movie filmmakers exploited and expanded on what had gone before. In the wake of *Halloween*, this meant – not to put too fine a point on it – more boobs and more blood. While critics generally praised *Halloween* for its restraint, its more exploitative elements were seized with gusto by filmmakers who wanted their slice of the slasher movie pie. They mixed stage blood, nudity, scares – and often cheese – in a crowd-pleasing way that is so often missing from today's anaemic genre offerings.

The explosion of the slasher movie was mainly – but not exclusively – an American and Canadian phenomena. Teenagers (and those pretending to be teens) were sliced

BATTLE OF THE SEXES

Despite women shedding their clothes in classic slasher movies, when up against a psycho with a machete, men were more at risk. In the 175 slasher films made between 1978 and 1984, some 558 of the 1,046 on-screen fatalities were male as opposed to 488 female deaths.

and diced in droves in high schools, dorms, summer camps and night schools. It's a wonder that a whole generation didn't just vanish in a blur of corn syrup, flashing blades and Farrah Fawcett hair.

Of course, *Halloween* may have kicked off this tidal wave of crimson, but it was not created in a cultural vacuum as this book shows. While I begin this chapter by looking at this iconic movie, I will also review it in the context of other key films of the Golden Age.

Below In the Golden Age there was no escape for anyone. A not-very-friendly clown advertises *The Funhouse*.

1978 – HALLOWEEN AND THE NIGHT HE CAME HOME

The Golden Age began in 1978 when John Carpenter created what is arguably the perfect horror movie. *Halloween* **secured Carpenter's future and launched the career of its young star, Jamie Lee Curtis.**

Above Donald Pleasence as Dr. Loomis in *Halloween*.

Influenced by a myriad of sources as diverse as the *giallo Blood and Black Lace,* the sci-fi film *Westworld* and the proto-slasher *Black Christmas, Halloween* would become the genre-defining work with only the slightest plot. The story centres around the murder by a six-year-old boy of his teenage sister on Halloween in 1963. Fifteen years later, the now adult Michael Myers breaks out of the asylum to return to his hometown of Haddonfield to resume his rampage on All Hallows Eve. His victims, seemingly chosen at random, are three high school girls. The increasingly crazed psychiatrist, Dr. Loomis, who had fought to keep him locked away for life, pursues Myers.

Irwin Yablans, one of the film's eventual executive producers, came up with the idea, originally thinking that it might

'What was living behind that boy's eyes was purely and simply . . . "evil".'

– Dr. Loomis on Michael Myers, *Halloween*

centre around babysitters terrorized by a psychopath (the project was originally titled *The Babysitter Murders*). Wanting to keep costs to a minimum, Yablans decided the film should take place over just one day and night. He chose to use Halloween: the scariest night of the year.

Left Iconic poster artwork for John Carpenter's seminal slasher movie.

THE TRICK WAS TO
STAY ALIVE

John Carpenter's

HALLOWEEN x

starring DONALD PLEASENCE and JAMIE LEE CURTIS

Presented by MOUSTAPHA AKKAD
Executive Producer IRWIN YABLANS   Produced by DEBRA HILL

Above British poster art for *Halloween*.

Yablans was already involved with Carpenter, having distributed his film *Assault on Precinct 13* (1976). While that film had failed to find an audience in the States, it struck a chord in England. A dejected Yablans had been persuaded to enter the film at the London Film Festival by the owner of the British film company Miracle Films, Michael Myers, the man whose name was later used for Carpenter's bogeyman as a mark of respect and thanks.

Yablans subsequently approached Carpenter with his concept for *The Babysitter Murders*. Carpenter was overjoyed with the prospect of directing the film as he needed a job, having just finished the TV thriller *Someone's Watching Me!* (1978). He had also become increasingly frustrated by the constraints put on him by the TV industry and was delighted to be promised final cut on the movie. Carpenter set to work on the script with his then girlfriend Debra Hill, who went on to produce the film. She told *Fangoria*:

We went back to the old idea of Samhain, that Halloween was the night where all the souls are let out to wreak havoc on the living, and then came up with the story about the most evil kid who ever lived. . . . We didn't want it to be gory. We wanted it to be like a jack-in-the-box.

It was these unashamed popcorn thrills that explains part of the reason why the film eventually resonated so powerfully with movie-goers. It was *the* golden formula aped by pretty much every slasher filmmaker who followed in Carpenter's giant footsteps.

The film was budgeted at a modest $300,000. Carpenter also agreed to write, direct, compose and perform the soundtrack for just $10,000 and a percentage of the profits. Backing was eventually secured from Arab financier Moustapha Akkad, who went on to be involved in all the *Halloween* sequels until his death in 2005.

Jamie Lee Curtis was chosen to play the virginal but ultimately resourceful Laurie Strode, partly because she was the daughter of *Psycho* star Janet Leigh. Carpenter had offered the role of Dr.

Loomis to Peter Cushing and Christopher Lee, who both turned it down (although Lee later said that was the biggest regret of his career); instead, it went to another great British thespian, Donald Pleasence. P. J. Soles had impressed Carpenter so much in *Carrie* (1976) that he had written the part of Laurie's classmate Lynda with her in mind. Nancy Kyes filled out the trio of ill-fated students as Annie.

'To make Myers frightening, I had him walk like a man, not a monster.'

– John Carpenter

Below Michael Myers haunts the night in *Halloween*.

Right Japanese promotional artwork for *Halloween* and (*far right*) alternative American artwork.

Halloween began shooting what was to be a tight and problematic four-week schedule in May 1978. Although set in the Midwest in autumn, it was actually filmed in California in the spring. Despite the trees being noticeably full and green, the production team used bags of specially painted brown leaves to give the right autumnal feel.

Playing the soon-to-be-iconic screen monster Michael Myers was Nick Castle, Carpenter's friend and budding director. Castle – who went on to direct the anaemic quasi slasher *TAG: The Assassination Game* (1982) – was the face of the adult Myers in all but one shot at the end of the film, when he is eventually unmasked. The look of Carpenter's 'the Shape' – the almost mythic figure who emerges from the darkness to claim his victims like a malevolent spider – could have ended up looking very different. Tommy Wallace – who was in charge of production design on the film – was sent to get the perfect mask for the role. The two choices were a clown and one made from a likeness of *Star Trek* actor William Shatner with the eyeholes cut larger and sprayed white. The moment he saw the Shatner mask, Carpenter knew that he had found the look for his bogeyman.

Perhaps the film's most famous scene is the opening shot of six-year-old Michael stalking his sister, who has just had sex with her boyfriend, through the Myers' home. The POV shot was achieved using a Panaglide camera that mimicked natural

HALLOWEEN

The trick is to stay alive.

Everyone is entitled to one good scare.

Below Spanish promotional artwork for *Halloween* and (*right*) Japanese artwork for the same movie.

movement. Michael's hands were, in fact, those of Debra Hill's. While looking as if it was filmed in one continuous shot, it was actually three shots cleverly edited together. Despite bearing a remarkable similarity to the opening sequence of the earlier *Blood and Lace* (see page 58), as already discussed, it is powerful and stylish, setting the scene both

thematically and visually for what was to come. This is due largely to the exquisite cinematography of Dean Cundey, who went on to work on many of Carpenter's subsequent films, including *The Fog* (1980) and *The Thing* (1982).

The horror genre has always mixed sex and violence, and *Halloween* is no exception. Although it is true that the virgin heroine survives while her sexually adventurous friends die, Carpenter, on one hand, denies that there is a conservative political agenda at play and states that sex-obsessed teenagers just pay less attention to their own personal safety. He has also said that Myers represents the revenge of the repressed. Whatever the truth, subsequent filmmakers copied what appeared to be a sex-equals-death mantra, probably because sex and death is a heady combination that sells movie tickets.

Surprisingly, *Halloween* very nearly didn't become a break-out, subgenre-defining film. Every major American studio – the same studios that would be rushing to claim their slice of the slasher-movie pie in the coming few years – declined to distribute it. In fact, Yablans scheduled a preview of the film and invited all the studios, but none even turned up. Carpenter showed it to an executive at 20th Century Fox minus the music score; she said that it just wasn't scary. Carpenter quickly realized that his minimal – and soon to become highly imitated – electronic score was the magic ingredient that perfectly complemented the visuals, helping generate ever-building fear and suspense.

Yablans decided to distribute the film via his own company, Compass International Pictures. Unlike most major films of today, *Halloween* débuted on limited release. Starting in Kansas City in October 1978, it opened in four theatres, at first causing few ripples at the box office. However, word of mouth proved to be the film's saviour. When it opened at the Chicago Film Festival in November 1978, the film literally exploded both commercially and critically.

Initially, not all the critics were positive. Influential *New Yorker* film critic Pauline Kael was scathing. However, her voice was in the minority. Tom Allen of the *Village Voice* said the film could 'stand proud alongside *Night of the Living Dead* and Hitchcock's *Psycho*'. Even Roger Ebert – who would go on to critically savage *Friday the 13th* two years later – praised the film as 'terrifying and creepy' and said that he would compare it with the classic slasher *Psycho*.

Halloween became a box-office phenomenon. It was one of the most profitable independent releases of all time, with an incredible $70 million world gross

Below The night *HE* came home . . .

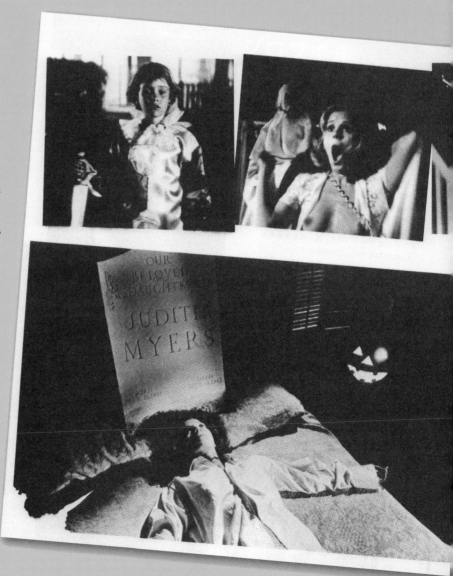

Below British video artwork for *Savage Water*.

Far right American poster art for *The Toolbox Murders*.

on its original release. It also unwittingly unleashed a tidal wave of blood that washed across both the big and small screen for the next six years and beyond.

OTHER FILMS RELEASED IN 1978

Before we get to the films that followed and emulated *Halloween,* let's take a look at some of the slashers that also appeared in that year. While many TV movies take their inspiration from big-screen successes, *Are You in the House Alone?* was first screened in American movie theatres just ahead of *Halloween.* Starring small-screen regular Kathleen Beller, it anticipated that film with its babysitter-in-peril motif, but the phantom phone calls suggest that *Black Christmas*

(see pages 60–61) might have been its inspiration. As with many films with slasher elements from around this time, they often catch modern viewers off guard, since the template for the slasher that we know and love had not yet been set.

Filmed in 1977 and released in March 1978, *The Toolbox Murders* has something of a fearsome reputation. Ostensibly based on a true story, it was actually the success of a re-release of *The Texas Chain Saw Massacre* that was the real genesis for the film. Sadly, it has none of the raw power of Tobe Hooper's film and none of the elegance of *Halloween*. What it does share with the latter film is psychotic evil exploding in suburbia – a deranged manager (played with relish by subgenre regular Cameron Mitchell) kills women in an apartment complex. But despite its sensationalist title, *The Toolbox Murders* is largely a tedious exercise in nonsuspense. As with *Are You in the House Alone?*, only the beginning section of the movie could be regarded as having true slasher elements.

While *Halloween* undeniably marked 1978 as the watershed year in the slasher genre, it also gave birth to what is possibly the worst slasher ever made – *Savage Water*. With a less-than-thrilling tale of boating on the white-water rapids of the Colorado River and murder and mayhem among a group of tourists, the film never gained a release in North America.

1979 – THE SLASHER COMES INTO ITS OWN

Perhaps surprisingly – given today's market, in which imitators of a potentially popular film can hit the shelves even before the original comes out – the opportunity to make money off the popularity of *Halloween* wasn't taken up by would-be slasher filmmakers as quickly as might be expected. Although many slashers went into production in 1979, they only really saw the light of day in 1980.

Below The flood of films began with the *Tourist Trap*.

The most interesting subgenre film released in 1979 was undoubtedly David Schmoeller's *Tourist Trap*. The plot of five teenagers getting lost and ending up at a bizarre wax museum whose owner is a psychopath is standard enough. However, the film quite literally comes alive as the teens are pursued by a mask-wearing killer (an obvious nod to *Halloween*) and the supernaturally animated mannequins controlled by the museum owner. Genuinely nightmarish, *Tourist Trap* also references sources as diverse as Stephen King's cult horror movie *Carrie* (1976) and Jean Cocteau's surrealist fairy tale *La belle et la bête* (1946).

Markedly less successful was *The Dark Ride*, a San Francisco–set serial killer opus that supposedly took its inspiration from the exploits of real-life murderer-rapist Ted Bundy. America was, at the time, in the throes of a love-hate relationship with real-life killers – outwardly condemning them but almost seeming to celebrate them through the constant glare of the media. The excellent character actor John Karlen, who plays the killer, lends the trashy proceedings a sense of gravitas it doesn't really warrant, however.

Ray Dennis Steckler's burlesque slasher movie, *The Hollywood Strangler Meets the Skid Row Slasher*, appears immune to *Halloween's* influences. This decidedly low-budget production has a rather staid,

EVERY YEAR YOUNG PEOPLE DISAPPEAR.

TOURIST TRAP

IRWIN YABLANS PRESENTS A COMPASS INTERNATIONAL/MANSON INTERNATIONAL RELEASE
CHARLES BAND PRODUCTIONS PRESENTS
TOURIST TRAP

Left Cheese and sleaze: Mexican lobby card combining *The Dark Ride* and *The Hollywood Strangler Meets the Skid Row Slasher*.

Below Video artwork for *The Hollywood Strangler Meets the Skid Row Slasher*.

Fangoria Magazine sez . . . "Tortured Thoughts". . . "Genuine Sleeze". . . —Thorn Brickshaw

NO ONE IS SAFE! FORREST DUKE

almost documentary-like approach to the on-screen mayhem. It at least has the novelty of two killers – one who strangles models and the other, a woman, who slashes tramps.

The homeless get a similarly raw deal in Abel Ferrara's infamous *The Driller Killer*, which is more of a riff on director Roman Polanski's *Repulsion* (1965) than a straightforward slasher. In both films, the main focus is on the internal turmoil of the killer rather than on their murderous deeds, although murders are certainly depicted; in the case of *The Driller Killer*, they are depicted so bloodily that the movie became one of the most infamous 'video nasties' in Britain.

More akin to *Halloween* was Fred Walton's *When a Stranger Calls* – although

THE BLOOD RUNS IN RIVERS...

...AND THE DRILL KEEPS TEARING THROUGH FLESH AND BONE

THE DRILLER KILLER

Starring: Carolyn Marz, Jimmy Laine & Baybi Day
Music by: Joseph Felia.
Directed by: Abel Ferrara. Produced by: Mavaron Films.
Running Time 84 Minutes

VIPCO

SEE WARNING ON REVERSE

"Unequivocally the most terrifying movie I've ever seen." —AFTER DARK Magazine

EVERY BABYSITTER'S NIGHTMARE BECOMES REAL...

WHEN A STRANGER CALLS

COLUMBIA PICTURES in association with MELVIN SIMON PRODUCTIONS presents
A BARRY KROST PRODUCTION
CHARLES DURNING   CAROL KANE   COLLEEN DEWHURST
WHEN A STRANGER CALLS
Also Starring TONY BECKLEY
RACHEL ROBERTS   RON O'NEAL   Executive Producers MELVIN SIMON AND BARRY KROST
Music by DANA KAPROFF   Written by STEVE FEKE and FRED WALTON
Produced by DOUG CHAPIN and STEVE FEKE   Directed by FRED WALTON
R RESTRICTED

Above left and right Blood and suspense: *The Driller Killer* and *When a Stranger Calls*.

Far right Final Girls: Linda Blair in *Hell Night* (top) and Jamie Lee Curtis in *Halloween* (bottom).

it went into production, coincidentally, just as *Halloween* wrapped. Based on the urban legend of a babysitter being tormented by a killer already lurking in the house, the film was an expansion of Walton's 20-minute short film, *The Sitter*, which was, in turn, most probably inspired by *Black Christmas*. Its roots show in the remarkably tense opening, which finds the babysitter (Carol Kane) being taunted by the killer (Tony Beckley), who repeatedly asks her, 'Have you checked the children?' The popularity of *Halloween* helped propel Walton's film

'Every babysitter's nightmare becomes real . . .'

– When a Stranger Calls

to an impressive $20,149,106 domestic box-office take.

Although the year 1979 produced a few classic slashers, it was in 1980 that the genre would really take off.

THE FINAL GIRL

Ever since Laurie Strode turned from shrinking wallflower to resourceful heroine in *Halloween*, it has become almost a cliché that a lone woman will be the only one left standing at the end of a slasher. Before *Halloween*, heroines had survived horror movies, but the climactic battle between Laurie and the bogeyman was a veritable blueprint of what was to follow. Sometimes there was a Final Boy (Alfred in *The Burning*), but that was a rarity.

The Final Girl (FG, as she became known) was, more often than not, a virgin (unlike most of her doomed friends). Shy but ultimately resourceful, she turns cat-and-mouse games to her advantage in her battle to make it to the closing credits. In many ways, the FG has taken over the role of the traditional male hero in slashers. Men are either relegated as machete fodder or fall by the wayside before the climactic battle ensues between the FG and the killer. While many aren't averse to screaming like banshees, they are also handy with a chainsaw or at hotwiring a getaway car.

Bucking the trend, some FGs – such as the one in *The Dorm That Dripped Blood* – make it through the movie but, in a cruel but ironic twist of fate, fall at the finish line. However, even if the FG does make it through to the end in one piece, there is sadly no guarantee that she will live through the sequel.

In the end, the resourceful, likeable and often androgynous FG appeals to both male and female viewers, and she continues to rise to the challenge of survival to this very day.

1980 – SUCCESS AND THE SLASHER

This was the year that the slasher movie really exploded into the public consciousness, with the incredible financial success of *Friday the 13th*.

The original Final Girl Jamie Lee Curtis told *Boxoffice* magazine that she thought the success of the slasher movie was a reaction to the 'boring' 1970s, saying, 'Watching people running from danger negates some of the apathy, even if it is only for 90 minutes'. However, this was also the year that former Hollywood star Ronald Reagan was elected as the 40th president of the United States – ushering in a new age of conservatism in America – and John Lennon was assassinated outside his apartment building in New York. The debate about the representation of women on-screen and the use of violence as entertainment also erupted, manifesting itself on the streets in the form of protests and boycotts. The slasher movie, at the height of its commercial powers, unwittingly found itself at the centre of this political and cultural maelstrom.

COURTING CONTROVERSY

Among the first films to appear in 1980 was the curiously meek *Silent Scream*, which looked back to the heyday of one of its stars – English actress Barbara Steele,

who had been the queen of Italian gothic horror in the 1960s – as much as it aped contemporary slasher movies. Steele plays a lobotomized ex-teen queen who escapes from the attic of a boarding house to carve up the students living there. It scared up a very respectable $15,800,000 at the domestic box office.

'If you're not back by midnight, you won't be coming home!'

– Prom Night

Two high-profile and thematically similar thrillers with slasher movie elements opened in early 1980. *Cruising* was directed by William Friedkin – most famous for directing *The Exorcist* (1973). Al Pacino plays a New York City cop sent undercover to catch the killer, who lurks in the city's leather bars. Featuring several brutal knife murders that wouldn't have looked out

TERROR SO SUDDEN THERE IS NO TIME TO SCREAM.

Silent Scream

against it after the erroneously labelled 'gay plague' broke out.

United Artists, which released the film, again tackled controversial subject matter with the little-seen *Windows*, which seemed to equate lesbianism with obsession and psychosis. A young divorcée (Talia Shire) suffers at the hands of her Sapphic neighbour, who arranges for her to be raped so that she can hear her moans on a tape recorder and who also kills anyone who gets between them. The film only played for a week or so before being hounded off screens and into obscurity by feminist groups. *Cruising* was a moderate hit for a high-profile movie, taking in $19,784,223, whereas *Windows* made just $2,128,395. Carrying on the decidedly grindhouse groove (with the exploitative elements and nudity overshadowing suspense) of many of the slasher movies made the previous year, *Don't Answer the Phone!* kicked off the legendary *Don't* cycle. The films in this series were unrelated apart from their titles.

Below Artwork for *Don't Answer the Phone!*

of place in a slasher, *Cruising* attracted controversy from the beginning. Shot in 1979, the film was dogged by protests from the city's gay community, who were unhappy with the way they were being portrayed, as the film seems to imply that both homosexuality and homicidal tendencies spread like a disease. Friedkin has denied that this was his intention.

Although the film predates the emergence of the AIDS crisis by over a year, some people argue that the negative portrayal of the gay community in the film helped fuel the subsequent backlash

RUN - if you must
HIDE - if you can
SCREAM but...

DON'T ANSWER THE PHONE!

X

.....**He'll Know You're Alone!**

Starring

¡NO ENTRES A LA CASA! LA MUERTE TE ESPERA
UN MANIATICO TE PUEDE CONVERTIR EN
ANTORCHA HUMANA...

MIGUEL ANGEL BARRAGAN
presenta a:
DAN GRIMALDI
ROBERT OSTH · RUTH DARDICK en

el MANIÁTICO

NO ENTRES A LA CASA

¡¡EL FUEGO
FUE UN INSTRUMENTO DE PLACER

DIST. POR CENTRO INDEPENDIENTE

DON'T GO
IN THE HOUS

Above and right
Mexican lobby card
and British video
art for *Don't Go in
the House.*

The name might have led audiences to think they were in for another riff on *Black Christmas* or *When a Stranger Calls*. What they got was an unrelenting exercise in misogyny, with a repellent Vietnam vet (Nicholas Worth) strangling lingerie-clad women in Los Angeles and then mutilating their bodies. Rather than create sympathetic characters – in the way that a film such as *Halloween* does, for example – it seems solely to dwell on the suffering of the exclusively female victims while also attempting to titillate the audience.

Much better, but no less grim, was Joseph Ellison's psychological terror movie, *Don't Go in the House*, where Danny (Dan Grimaldi), who was abused by his mother as a child, loses his mind upon her death and traps and sets fire to women in a specially constructed metal room. Like

Norman Bates, Danny continues to hear his mother's voice – her criticism follows him from the grave. Despite being apples and oranges, *Don't Go in the House* played some theatres at the same time as *Friday the 13th*, although the former's tale of madness and the progeny of child abuse was an altogether darker proposition. It gives *Psycho* a grindhouse makeover (in one scene the camera lingers as a woman writhes graphically in the flames while hanging in chains from the ceiling). Perhaps unsurprisingly, *Don't Go in the House* was prosecuted as a 'video nasty' in the United Kingdom.

FRIDAY THE 13TH AND THE TURNING OF THE TIDE

Of all the slashers from this period, apart from *Halloween*, *Friday the 13th* (explored in depth on page 107) is probably the best known. Some may dismiss it as a popcorn movie, but it is a highly successful example of the subgenre, not just in revenue (it grossed an impressive $39,754,601 in the US alone) but also in terms of what it set out to do – to frighten and gross out the audience in equal measure and to entertain. However, while it is tempting to look back with tinted glasses at the slasher movies of the early 1980s and imagine that they were all warmly received on release, the slasher has rarely been looked on favourably by mainstream critics, and never was this more so the case than with *Friday the 13th*.

The main bone of contention for critics appeared to be that a major studio, Paramount, had 'lowered' itself to release this violent, independent picture onto thousands of screens across America.

Most vocal in their condemnation of the film were American review double-act Siskel and Ebert. So incensed were they that they gave away the shock ending of the film in an unsuccessful attempt to hurt its box-office takings. More controversially, they also encouraged movie fans to voice their disapproval by writing to Betsy Palmer, who played the psychotic Mrs. Voorhees in the film and previously had been best known for girl-next-door roles.

The Motion Picture Association of America (MPAA) was also criticized for allowing the film to pass with an R rating,

Below Friday the 13th *split opinions as well as faces* (left)*; American poster art for Sean Cunningham's hugely successful movie* (right)*.*

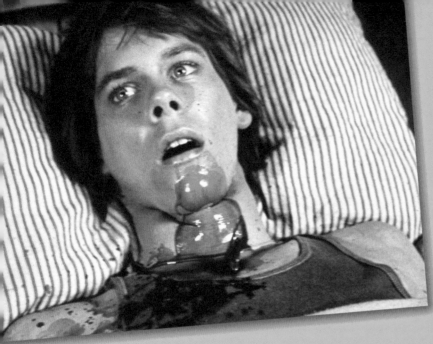

Although it shares the backwoods setting of the former film, *The Prey* is a far less successful venture. Featuring teenage campers who are stalked by a towering, deformed mountain man, regrettably, it is bogged down by a slow pace and pastoral scenery, including endless wildlife stock footage and a five-minute ukulele solo! It fails to excite, which probably explains its relative obscurity. The film was acquired by New World Pictures and heavily edited before being re-released briefly to theatres several years later in 1984.

Above **Kevin Bacon's character in** *Friday the 13th* **was the archetypal pot-smoking, horny teen victim.**

Right **British video artwork for** *Night of the Demon.*

as it had only a few minor cuts. It was a move they regretted when subsequent slasher filmmakers held up Sean S. Cunningham's film as a barometer of what were acceptable levels of violence for audiences to see. The MPAA, once burnt, twice shy and now sensitive to the criticism of the subgenre from everyone from film critics to women's groups, vowed to be much less lenient in the future – something that would eventually play a part in emasculating the slasher movie and lead to its, albeit temporary, demise.

The Prey was a contemporary of *Friday the 13th* and was shot in the autumn of 1979 but barely released in 1980.

'Doomed! You're all doomed!'

– Crazy Ralph, *Friday the 13th*

Warning–this film contains scenes of extreme and explicit violence

NIGHT OF THE DEMON

IFS

CHRISTMAS EVIL

A brilliant new chiller from IFS . . .

In Harry's eyes, there are good girls and bad girls. It's Christmas 1947 and the girls who have been bad are in real trouble... Certificate X.

IFS Video, Pinewood Studios, Iver, Bucks. SL0 0NH. Tel: (0753) 655011

spree. Made in New Jersey and Queens, it was barely released at the time – and audiences expecting another *Halloween* clone were not sure what to make of this slow-placed oddity. It works better as a bizarre black comedy than a slasher film – something that Jackson fully intended. Sadly, the director never got to make his mooted Easter Bunny slasher.

If you had to guess what kind of slasher movie David Hess (who played the main villain in Wes Craven's unrelentingly nasty *The Last House of the Left*) would make, it would probably not be the one he directed in 1980. Very low budget (just $78,000), the surprisingly cheesy *To All a Goodnight* has teenagers at a girl's finishing school threatened by another psycho dressed as Santa Claus. While boasting good special effects by Mark Shostrom, they are almost impossible to see in an all-pervading visual murkiness. Haphazardly edited,

Left and below
Video artwork for
Christmas Evil and
To All a Goodnight.

On a decidedly similar theme is James C. Wasson's enjoyably bad Bigfoot opus, *Night of the Demon* (not to be confused with Jacques Tourneur's 1957 occult classic). A borderline slasher movie, the action includes an anthropology student disembowelled and whipped with his own intestines and two girl scouts forced by the monster to stab each other in a bizarre and bloody dance of death. Perhaps unsurprisingly, the British police didn't see the funny side, and the film garnered undeserved notoriety as a 'video nasty'.

Originally titled *You Better Watch Out*, Lewis Jackson's *Christmas Evil* has a man so obsessed with the festive season that he takes to dressing as Santa and checking which kids have been naughty or nice. He eventually snaps and embarks on a killing

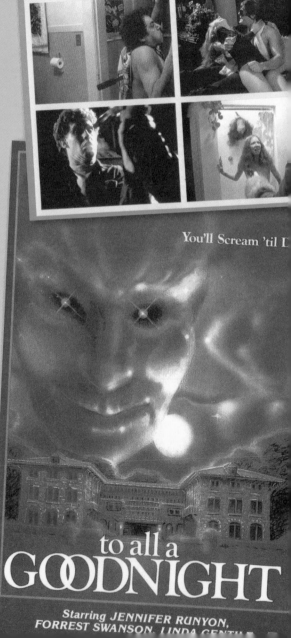

You'll Scream 'til D

to all a GOODNIGHT

Starring JENNIFER RUNYON,
FORREST SWANSON, LINDA GENTIL

Below Male victims in *Home Sweet Home* (*left*) and *Prom Night* (*right*).

the movie features abundant clichés, with one girl whimpering, 'We're going to die. . . . We're all going to DIE!'. It foreshadows the dorm slashers of the following year. It didn't receive a theatrical release but did good business on video. The producer of Hess's film was Sandy Cobe, who also produced the rock slasher *Terror on Tour* in 1980; most of Cobe's films followed the same pattern as that of *To All a Goodnight*, as they did well on video.

Cobe was also involved in the abysmal *Home Sweet Home* (1980). With a tagline that promised, 'This year, it's not the turkey being carved for Thanksgiving', the plot centres round a giggling, psychotic bodybuilder on PCP (American TV fitness personality Jake Steinfeld), who runs over an old lady before killing off a group of friends and family at a remote ranch.

THE CANADIAN BOOM

It wasn't just America that was reaping the benefits of the slasher, however. A boom in Canadian slasher movies at the time was due to the undeniably winning financial formula of *Halloween* coupled with good tax-break incentives that saw genre production booming north of the border.

Jamie Lee Curtis returned to the subgenre in the Canadian-produced film *Prom Night* (for more on the film, see page 191). It cemented her reputation as Scream Queen – even if she did dub it 'Disco Death'.

Director Paul Lynch, who also directed *Humongous* (1982), was keen not to miss out on the boom. His first proposal was the aborted *Don't Go See the Doctor!* about an insane gynecologist, but he persevered and picked a prom night as an undeniably fertile ground for a slasher.

emos
gún día...

hor de Dios,
ea así!

JAKE STEINFELD
SALLEE ELYSE

PETER DE PAULA
COLLETTE TRUGG

Guión: THOMAS BUSH
RICHARD TUFO   Dirección: NETTIE PEÑA

EL INVITADO DEL DIABLO
"HOME SWEET HOME"

If you're not back by midnight... you won't be coming home!

PROM NIGHT

A SIMCOM PRODUCTION
LESLIE NIELSEN • JAMIE LEE CURTIS in "P
SCREENPLAY BY WILLIAM GRAY • STORY BY R
PRODUCED BY PETER SIMPSON • DIRECTED B
AVCO EMBASSY PICTURES Release

Riding on the coattails of *Friday the 13th*, *Prom Night* was a sizable hit, raking in nearly $15 million on a modest budget of just $1.6 million.

DE PALMA AND *DRESSED TO KILL*

Brian De Palma had already veered into proto-slasher territory with *Sisters*. A noted follower of Hitchcock as well as Stanley Kubrick (who had directed the cerebral Stephen King psycho-shocker *The Shining* in the same year), De Palma was one of the first mainstream directors to see the cinematic potential of mixing the now-traditional spills of the psycho-thriller with the contemporary edge of the modern slasher movie.

De Palma's *Dressed to Kill,* starring Michael Caine and Nancy Allen, was heavily influenced by *Psycho* and includes a now-familiar shower sequence and a transvestite murderer, although the film's gory and violent razor attacks are far more graphic than Hitchcock could have gotten away with in the 1960s.

Unfortunately for De Palma, *Dressed to Kill* initiated a huge wave of protest on both sides of the Atlantic from women's groups deeply unhappy with the rise in popularity of what they perceived as violent 'women-in-peril' films.

De Palma was roundly labelled a misogynist by feminist protesters. The National Organization for Women (NOW) and members of other feminist organizations took part in a silent picket of the film when it was shown on the

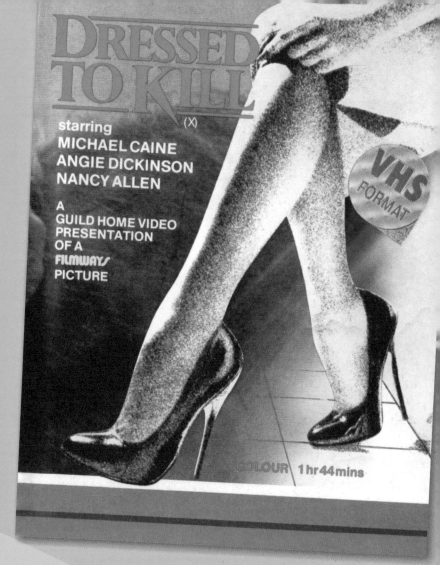

Above British video cover for *Dressed to Kill.*

University of Iowa campus. In May 1982, the National Film Theatre (NFT) in London was similarly picketed by feminists at a showing of the movie during a women's film season. The celebratory banner 'Women Live' was changed to read 'Women Slashed and Murdered at the NFT'.

However, despite the controversy, and proving without a doubt that the subgenre was at the top of its game, the film took almost $32 million at the domestic box office on its release.

Below and right
Promotional artwork
for *Phobia* and
*He Knows You're
Alone.*

SLASHER ALUMNI

Considerably less successful was John Huston's *Phobia*. The talented director – who had made the excellent *Wise Blood* the year before and had directed a number of Hollywood classics – seemed particularly ill at ease with a modern horror thriller. Despite a good premise – patients attend therapy to beat their phobias only to end up dying because of them – it is unfeasibly dull. More fun than actually watching the film is spotting the slasher movie alumni dotted throughout this Canadian production. Future *Happy Birthday to Me* cast members Lisa Langlois and David Eisner play ill-fated patients, and Marian Waldman, who was such a joy to watch as the boozy sorority mother in *Black Christmas*, puts in a brief appearance as Mrs. Casey in her last film role before her death in 1985.

Armand Mastroianni's *He Knows You're Alone*, in which an insane man (Tom Rolfing) targets brides-to-be after being jilted for another man, is a slavish imitator of *Halloween*. It has an identikit soundtrack and a similar-sounding location (compare Westfield to *Halloween*'s Haddonfield). The Dr. Loomis character is the husband-to-have-been of the first victim and the killer pops up in the shot just like Michael Myers. However, despite Mastroianni fluffing many of the false scares, there's still much to enjoy here. As in most early 1980s slasher movies, the killer does not actually wear a mask. Perhaps taking a lead from *When A Stranger Calls*, Rolfing grotesquely contorts his face and is a genuinely creepy presence.

Caitlin O'Heaney is a likable Final Girl (see box on page 85). The prologue – where a young woman is murdered while watching a slasher film at the cinema – is perhaps a comment on the differences

But this time...
there's good reason!

He Knows You're Alone

METRO-GOLDWYN-MAYER Presents **"HE KNOWS YOU'RE ALONE"** A LANSBURY/BERUH PRODUCTION
Starring DON SCARDINO · CAITLIN O'HEANEY Music by ALEXANDER and MARK PESKANOV
Co-Producers ROBERT DI MILIA and NAN PEARLMAN · Director of Photography GERALD FEIL
Executive Producers EDGAR LANSBURY and JOSEPH BERUH · Written by SCOTT PARKER
Produced by GEORGE MANASSE · Directed by ARMAND MASTROIANNI
R · MGM · United Artists

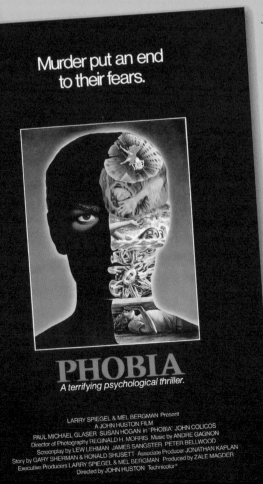

Murder put an end
to their fears.

PHOBIA
A terrifying psychological thriller.

LARRY SPIEGEL & MEL BERGMAN Present
A JOHN HUSTON FILM
PAUL MICHAEL GLASER SUSAN HOGAN in ``PHOBIA' JOHN COLICOS
Director of Photography REGINALD H. MORRIS Music by ANDRE GAGNON
Screenplay by LEW LEHMAN JAMES SANGSTER PETER BELLWOOD
Story by GARY SHERMAN & RONALD SHUSETT Associate Producer JONATHAN KAPLAN
Executive Producers LARRY SPIEGEL & MEL BERGMAN Produced by ZALE MAGDER
Directed by JOHN HUSTON Technicolor®

between reel and real violence and was seemingly the inspiration for a similar scene in *Scream 2* (1997). It is also notable for Tom Hanks making his film début in a slasher movie as a jogger who escapes with his life. The independent feature was shot for a mere $300,000 on Staten Island in New York in the winter of 1979. After the success that Paramount had with *Friday the 13th*, most major studios were keen to cash in on the slasher movie craze, and much to the surprise of the filmmakers themselves, MGM snapped up the rights for a cool $2 million. The film was a modest hit for the studio, making around $5 million at the domestic box office.

In David Paulsen's *Schizoid*, attending therapy is also fraught with danger, with patients from the group falling victim to a scissor-wielding killer. Paulsen had made the proto-slasher *Savage Weekend*

but seemed intent on making a straight thriller – albeit a sleazy one – with a few slasher movie trappings. It is ably enlivened by the presence of the eccentric actor Klaus Kinski. *Schizoid* also features an early performance by Christopher Lloyd as a creepy boiler maintenance man.

Jamie Lee Curtis returned to Canada and the subgenre yet again with *Terror Train* (see page 191 for review) in which a fast-moving graduation bash aboard a train turns deadly when a demented killer comes along for the ride. Despite the presence of Curtis, the film was only a meagre success, taking in $8 million at the domestic box office on a $3.5 million budget. It was not a disaster but probably less than 20th Century Fox was hoping for, and it was certainly less than the two previous Curtis slashers had made. Despite the slasher film being at the height of its popularity, murmuring began that the subgenre was already burning itself out.

Above and left
American poster art for *Terror Train* and British video artwork for *Schizoid*.

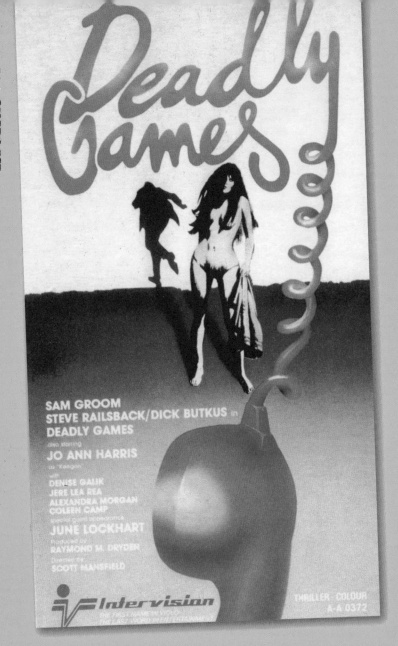

Above British video cover for *Deadly Games*.

'. . . a tale of slasher deaths at the hands of a vengeful spirit . . .'

sister's friends. It seems as if slasher movie elements have been inserted into what is an otherwise routine thriller purely because the film's backers presumed audiences wanted them there. Despite this, *Deadly Games* appears to have sat on the shelf until 1982.

Ulli Lommel, a German director and one-time collaborator with art house auteur Rainer Werner Fassbinder (whose films include 1981's *Lola* and 1982's *Querelle*), made the unlikely switch from art films – his acclaimed and disturbing *Tenderness of the Wolves* (*Die Zärtlichkeit der Wölfe*, 1973) is about a serial killer who targets young boys – to commercially orientated American slasher movies with *The Boogeyman*.

Despite a meagre budget, *The Boogeyman* – a tale of slasher deaths at the hands of a vengeful spirit – was filmed in a very handsome way in Maryland in 1979. From its opening panning shot of a house at night, it is clear that the film's primary inspiration – both visually and thematically – was *Halloween*. To cover all horror bases (and to boost its commercial appeal),

THE LURE OF THE SLASHER

Scott Mansfield's *Deadly Games* is a perfect example of how the slasher influenced the modern thriller in the early 1980s. A music journalist returns home after the death of her sister, but she slowly realizes that it wasn't an accidental death after a masked killer begins attacking her dead

THE BOGEY MAN

VIPCO
present

Suzanna Love · Ron James · John Carradine

Left The British video cover for *The Bogey Man* (with a different spelling from the American release) that may have helped it end up on the 'video nasty' list.

Below Lesleh Donaldson hides from the killer in this Mexican lobby card for *Funeral Home.*

Far right American poster art for *New Year's Evil.*

Lommel makes sure to use a house that is also a dead ringer for the one used in *The Amityville Horror* (1979).

Fish-out-of-water directors often produce interesting work, and this is the case with *The Boogeyman.* The meeting of European and North American styles and sensibilities gives the film an otherworldly, if sometimes stilted, feel. Despite starting out as a straight example of the subgenre, *The*

Boogeyman quickly veers into supernatural territory, which was unusual at the time, although it became more commonplace later on. Again echoing *Halloween*, the film uses many POV shots, although the killer doesn't appear in a physical sense. Rather the vengeful spirit causes people to kill themselves or causes violent accidents. The use of a noncorporeal slasher villain may have influenced the popular *Final*

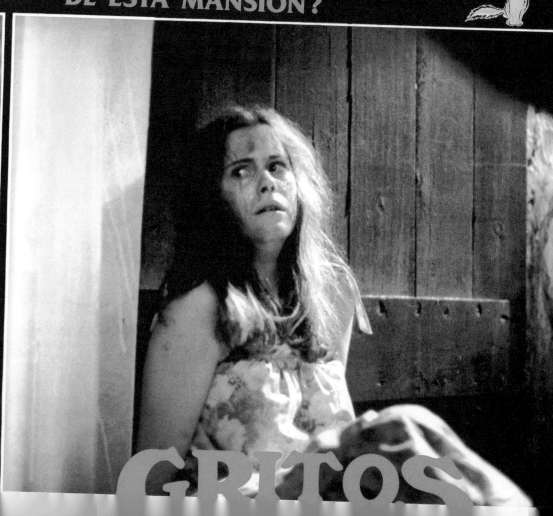

QUE TERRIBLE SECRETO ENCIERRA EL SOTANO DE ESTA MANSION ?

GRITOS EN LA NOCHE

KAY HAWTREY
BARRY MORSE
HARVEY ATKIN
Dirección WILLIAM FRUET

GRITOS

Destination series (in which teenagers are also killed by a similarly unseen Grim Reaper in outrageously inventive ways) in the 2000s.

The Boogeyman reputedly earned $25 million globally on a budget of less than half a million dollars. Unfortunately, it was another slasher movie that ran into the 'video nasty' hysteria that gripped the United Kingdom in the early 1980s.

Released in October in its native Canada (but not making its United States début until 1982) was William Fruet's *Funeral Home*. Future subgenre star Lesleh Donaldson gets her first and only leading role as a Nancy Drew–like teenager who goes to stay with her weird grandmother who has turned her funeral home into a guest house – only to find the guests are mysteriously vanishing. It became a big cult hit in Mexico, leading Donaldson to rival Jamie Lee Curtis in the scream-queen stakes south of the border.

Significant dates on the calendar were fast being used up as hooks for new slasher films, as were the techniques to make the plots more interesting. Just as *Prom Night* had attempted to mix slasher movie thrills with disco, *New Year's Evil* tried, far less successfully, with New Wave music. In the film, a female rock TV host is stalked by a psycho who calls himself 'Evil' and phones to say that he will kill someone each time midnight strikes in the different time zones across the United States. Despite its novel approach, *New Year's Evil* is dull and practically goreless. Worst of all, it has

Right This Mexican lobby card emphasizes the explicit violence in *Maniac*.

a depressing streak of misogyny running through it – with a lengthy diatribe by 'Evil' about why all women are 'sluts and need to be punished'.

At the tail end of 1980, however, came one of the most controversial slasher movies of all time, William Lustig's *Maniac*. Joe Spinell is particularly effective as the twitchy serial killer who randomly stalks and scalps women in New York; he sees this as justifiable revenge for the abuse that he suffered at the hands of his own mother. In an unlikely twist, he also starts dating a beautiful fashion photographer played by Caroline Munro. The *New York Times* wasn't impressed, however, and critic Vincent Canby sneered that watching Spinell act like a psychopathic killer with a mother complex was like 'watching someone else throw up'.

Maniac was quite possibly the most explicit slasher movie to date. Tom Savini – who had orchestrated the bloody violence in *Friday the 13th* – upped the ante here. But it was the unrelenting graphic violence against women that proved to be the most problematic factor when releasing it: the film was so nihilistic and violent that Lustig decided to release it unrated to American screens, thereby essentially sidestepping the MPAA. The controversy around the film resulted in *Maniac* grossing around $6 million in the United States. It didn't get a chance in the United Kingdom – the British Board of Film Classification rejected the film outright for a theatrical release in July 1981.

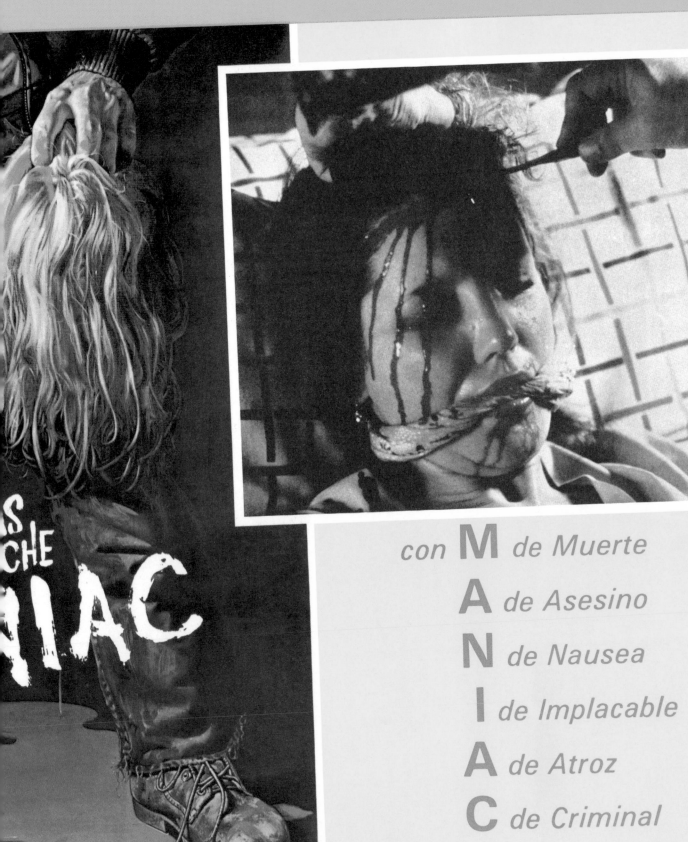

con **M** de Muerte

A de Asesino

N de Nausea

I de Implacable

A de Atroz

C de Criminal

'Maniac' con Joe Spinell · Caroline Munro

1981 – THE SLASHER AT ITS PEAK?

By 1981 the subgenre was showing signs that its audiences were approaching saturation point. Films such as *My Bloody Valentine* all but bombed at the box office despite heavy advertising; other films continued to turn a healthy profit.

Slashers were still relatively cheap to make, and so the crimson tsunami continued in the eternal search for the next *Halloween* or *Friday the 13th*.

Released on New Year's Day 1981, Jeff Lieberman's *Just Before Dawn* is an arrestingly different take on the campers-in-peril slasher movie, during which a group of youngsters are murdered by an oddball backwoods family. Like Michael Myers in *Halloween*, the killers here – inbred twin brothers (both played by John Hunsaker) – are merely ciphers, shambling hunks of meat, giggling killing machines with no rhyme or reason for their crimes. They are jarringly at odds with the teenagers whose only concern is disco dancing around the campfire, skinny-dipping and discussing makeup.

The woods provide both a benign and intimidating backdrop to this potent juxtaposition. Veteran actor George Kennedy is a scream as the ranger, who talks to his plants and horse and dead-pans to the doomed teenagers, 'At least tell me where you're going so when you don't come back, I'll know how to fill out the report.' *Just Before Dawn* is capped with an

'Beware of what you make fun of, you little asshole.'

– Happy, *My Bloody Valentine*

unforgettable, once-seen-never-forgotten dénouement, when Constance (Deborah Benson) – the film's Final Girl – takes the expected 'fight back' scene to a whole new level of shocking absurdity.

Also released at the beginning of 1981 was *The Outing*, about a group of people stranded in a ghost town who are killed off one by one. Unfortunately, this low-budget

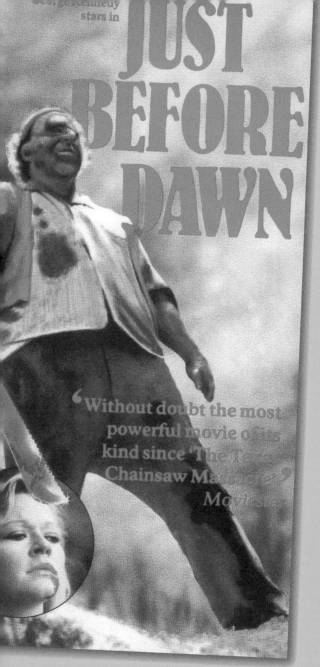

Without doubt the most powerful movie of its kind since 'The Texas Chainsaw Massacre'
Movie Star

Left British video-cover art for *Just Before Dawn*.

MY BLOODY VALENTINE AND CENSORSHIP

One of the best and most fondly remembered subgenre films from this era – and released just in time for lovers everywhere to cuddle just a little bit closer – *My Bloody Valentine* hit the screens in February of 1981 (see page 195 for more).

After the major box-office success of the previous year's *Friday the 13th*, Paramount decided to see if lightning really could strike twice and picked up the Canadian production. Produced by André Link and John Dunning and directed by Hungarian filmmaker George Mihalka, together they fashioned one of the most iconic slashers of the period.

My Bloody Valentine was actually released in a highly edited version after being rejected in its original form by the Motion Picture Association of America, threatening it with an X rating and therefore commercial death. In trying to outdo the excesses of *Friday the 13th*, the makers had incensed the censor.

Mihalka blamed the backlash against violent movies on the murder of John Lennon in December 1980. He told website Bloody-disgusting.com: 'We were the first up in front of the MPAA. The response was, "Forget it. This is an X." Especially in those days, that would have meant going from a 1,200-theatre release to about 60 porno theatres'.

With such a tight editing deadline, the filmmakers had no choice but to bow to the censor's demands – something that may have led to the film's initial less-than-

bore is a stultifying exercise in tedium. Only of interest is its alternative title *Scream* (a full 15 years before Wes Craven's film) and that it is one of the first slasher movies to have a supernatural angle and one of the only slashers not to have any female victims.

There's more than one way
to lose your heart...

MY BLOODY VALENTINE

RESTRICTED R

spectacular financial success. *My Bloody Valentine* made just $6 million, a sizable return on a budget of $1.5 to $2.5 million but much less than Paramount had hoped for, given the profits made on *Friday the 13th*.

MOPPING UP THE BLOOD

Warner Bros. picked up the independently produced *Eyes of a Stranger* for release. While not quite as mean-spirited as the previous year's *Don't Answer the Phone!*, it doesn't win any prizes for tact. A TV anchorwoman reporting on a series of murders begins to suspect that her neighbour may be the culprit.

The film shuffles from one suspense-free scene to another, bathed in the pastel nihilistic look – the result of the blistering Miami sunshine, cheap film stock and a bad video transfer – that typified many early 1980s genre flicks. Despite employing Tom Savini – in the hope that he might bring some of his *Friday the 13th* magic to this mess – most of his graphic special effects ended up on the cutting-room floor. Jennifer Jason Leigh makes a spirited early appearance as a deaf, mute and blind teenager and sister of the lead.

Despite featuring that old slasher movie standby – the gruesomely severed head in a fish tank – it barely made $1 million at the box office.

Faring little better was *Night School*, a tale of women being decapitated at a Boston college, which was released outside America as *Terror Eyes*. Among all early American slasher films, *Night School* seems the most influenced by the Italian *giallo* – from the less-than-riveting police investigation to stealing the killer's crash-helmet disguise and gender from Andrea Bianchi's *Strip Nude for Your Killer*. Although banned in the United Kingdom as a 'video nasty', it isn't that explicitly

Ha Asesinado Muchas Mujeres. No Se Dejará La Próxima Matar

OJOS ASESINOS
(Eyes of a Stranger)

Distribuida por

Una Warner Comm

Above Jennifer Jason Leigh in *Eyes of a Stranger*.

Far left Mining a rich vein of terror: American promotional artwork for *My Bloody Valentine*.

'Blistering Miami sunshine, cheap film stock and a bad video transfer . . .'

A is for Apple
B is for Bed
C is for Coed
D is for Dead
F is for Failing
to keep your head

NIGHT SCHOOL

A LESSON IN TERROR

LORIMAR PRESENTS "NIGHT SCHOOL"
LEONARD MANN · RACHEL WARD · DREW SNYDER · JOSEPH R. SICARI
Executive Producers MARC GREGORY COM JEAN and BERNARD KEBADJIAN
Written by RUTH AVERGON · Produced by LARRY BABB AND RUTH AVERGON
Directed by KEN HUGHES · A RESOURCE PRODUCTION
A PARAMOUNT PICTURE
LORIMAR   Copyright ©MCMLXXXI By Paramount Pictures Corporation. All Rights Reserved

R RESTRICTED
UNDER 17 REQUIRES ACCOMPANYING
PARENT OR ADULT GUARDIAN

Above and right American poster artwork for *Night School* and promotional Japanese flyer for *The Funhouse*.

violent. It is the film's misanthropy and perhaps misogyny (despite both the screenwriter and the killer being women) that probably caused British censors to baulk at it.

Universal Studios – which will forever be remembered for its creature features of the 1930s – tried to mix its past glories and the slasher movie with Tobe Hooper's *The Funhouse*, when teenagers decide to spend the night at the carnival, not knowing that a hideously deformed man lurks in the shadows (see full review on page 199). Despite a reportedly troubled production, this teens-in-peril opus still managed $8 million at the box office.

Bloody Birthday distinguished itself by casting the knife-wielding marauders as a trio of cherubic-faced school children. In decidedly bad taste – and all the more fun for it – the little darlings shoot, hack and whack their way through the open-mouthed cast. Made in 1980, the film was barely released as *Hide and Go Kill* in February 1981. As happened with many subgenre films at the time, it was reissued

under a different title – this time *Creeps* in January 1982 – to lure a fresh audience.

Students had been offed at prom night with varying degrees of success, but now some wouldn't make it to *Graduation Day* either. Arguably the cheesiest of all the early 1980s slashers, the film finds a killer picking off members of a sports team and features a kung-fu-fighting Final Girl. One teenager gets a makeshift sword tracheotomy while shaving her legs in a

BLOODY BIRTHDAY

Starring:
LORI LETHIN   MELINDA CORDELL   JULIE BROWN
With SUSAN STRASBERG as Miss Davis
And Special Appearance by JOSÉ FERRER as The Doctor
Screenplay by ED HUNT and BARRY PEARSON
Produced by GERALD T. OLSON Directed by ED HUNT

IVER FILM SERVICES
THE PROFESSIONALS AT PINEWOOD

IFS

Left and below
British video artwork
for *Bloody Birthday*
and American
poster artwork for
Graduation Day.

sink, while another falls on a bed of spikes. Their faces are then crossed off the team photo with lipstick. Orchestrated by one of the only women working in the horror special-effects field at the time – Jill Rockow – the gore effects are terrible, with the fakest-looking decapitation since Herschel Gordon Lewis laid down his camera.

The film is directed with some disdain by Herb Freed. On a meagre $250,000 budget, it topped the box office in L.A. before a profitable regional run.

ONE GOOD SLASH DESERVES ANOTHER – FRIDAY THE 13TH PART 2

Released around the same time was *Friday the 13th Part 2*. Paramount figured that

even a decapitated villain couldn't dent its plans to wring more money out of Sean Cunningham's remarkably successful slasher movie formula. Cunningham wanted to move on to other things, so he passed the directorial reins to Steve Miner. Slicker and better paced than the original, *Friday the 13th Part 2* is perhaps what the quintessential early 1980s slasher movie is all about. Despite employing almost every cliché known to man, the film succeeds perhaps because of – not despite – its familiarity. It is certainly ably helped by what many regard as the best Final Girl of the period, Amy Steel. As Ginny Field, she is warm, resourceful and plucky, the perfect foil for Jason Voorhees, who is now fully grown and is out to revenge his mother's death. The film takes place five years after the first, with a fresh crop of counsellors being stalked and offed in inventive ways at a camp near the now-abandoned Camp Crystal Lake. If it sounds familiar, writer Ron Kurz knew not to mess with a successful formula. The

There are 200 seniors a
Midvale High.
And seven days 'til gradua

GRADUATION DAY

The Class of '81 is running out of tim

"GRADUATION DAY" Starring CHRISTOPHER GEORGE and PATCH MACKENZ
Introducing E. DANNY MURPHY, MICHAEL PATAKI and E.J. PEAKER as "Blondi
Screenplay by ANNE MARISSE and HERB FREED Story by DAVID BAUGHN
Director of Photography DANIEL YARUSSI Produced by DAVID BAUGHN and HERB FREE

Below and right The simple but effective artwork used for *Friday the 13th Part 2* (*below*). An unlucky camper in the same movie.

Opposite page American poster art for *The Burning* (*far right*) and a moment of terror from the same film (*bottom*).

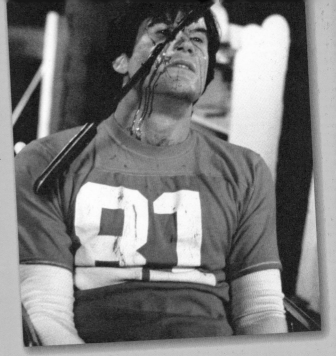

sequel – if not a direct remake – utilizes similar themes.

Unsurprisingly, critic Roger Ebert, who savaged the first film, wasn't any more impressed with the sequel, saying, 'Two dozen movies a year feature a mad killer going berserk. . . . They're all as bad as this one'.

Fans were disappointed by the severely truncated special effects – surely the raison d'être of *Friday the 13th* – cut at the behest of the US censors still smarting over the criticism they received for letting the original through relatively unscathed.

Still, *Friday the 13th Part 2* made nearly $22 million at the domestic box office. Although it was just over half of what the original had taken the previous year, it was still a huge profit on a relatively small outlay of just over a million dollars.

THE BURNING

Suffering similarly brutal censorship at the behest of the MPAA was the almost thematically identical *The Burning,* in which Cropsy, a hideously

burned caretaker at Camp Blackfoot, goes after teenagers with garden shears. *The Burning* was made for around $1.5 million but barely made a mark at the box office (see a full review on page 192).

Janet Maslin said in the *New York Times* that *The Burning* follows 'the one-dead-teen-per-15-minutes-of-screen-time formula'. Jimmy Summers, writing in the June 1981 issue of *Boxoffice* magazine, admitted that the film was one of the 'best performed of the genre' but 'one of the sickest of the recent string of gore fests'.

BUILDING ON PREVIOUS SUCCESSES

If the idea of screen legend Elizabeth Taylor appearing in a slasher movie seemed far-fetched (reportedly she considered a role in *The Fan*), then Lauren Bacall must seem an equally unlikely candidate. Bacall eventually appeared as the aging Broadway actress stalked by an obsessed fan (a young Michael Biehn). Showing the all-permeating influence of the slasher movie, *The Fan* flirts with more exploitative elements – notably the 'How would you like to be fucked with a meat cleaver?' dialogue (which was subsequently removed for the film's DVD release). However, in its efforts to remain classy – i.e., dull – the film fails to generate much in the way of real tension. Despite its failings, it still managed to make over $3 million at the box office.

HAPPY BIRTHDAY TO ME

A film that had no qualms about remaining believable was the enjoyably loopy Canadian-lensed *Happy Birthday to Me* – in which students at an exclusive school are bumped off one by one before the 18th birthday of Virginia, played by Melissa Sue Anderson (see a full review on page 194). Although made before *My Bloody Valentine* – and sharing the same producers, John Dunning and André Link – it was released three months later. The rights were bought

THORN EMI VIDEO

HAND M

JEAN UBAUD, MICHAEL COHL and CORKY BUR present a MIRAMAX Production of

THE BURNING

Starring
BRIAN MATTHEWS
LEAH AYERS
BRIAN BACKER
LARRY JOSHUA
and LOU DAVID
as Cropsy

he most frightening of all maniac films

SIX OF THE MOST BIZARR

John will n
eat shish ke
again

PRAY YOU'RE NOT I

Above and right
British video art
for *The Fan* and
the British cinema
artwork for *Happy
Birthday to Me*.

by Columbia, keen to get a piece of the slasher movie box-office action – and they were rewarded with a modest hit.

Reading the press pack, nowhere is the 'S' word mentioned; rather, the film is heavily promoted as a 'psychological mystery shocker'. Despite this, it follows the slasher movie formula closely, with the promotional ad sensationally promising audiences 'six of the most bizarre murders you'll ever see'. *Happy Birthday to Me* is best remembered for its mask-ripping finale. It was originally slapped with an X rating and had to get rid of its excessively bloodier moments before earning an R rating. It still made around $10 million at the box office.

FINAL EXAM

More students hit the floor in the slasher-cum-frat-boy humour hybrid *Final Exam*, in which teenagers are stalked and stabbed by an anonymous killer. It was made in North Carolina at the tail end of 1979 but remained on the shelf for over a year. It

...RDERS YOU WILL EVER SEE.

Steven will never ride a motorcycle again.
Greg will never lift weights again.
Who's killing the school's snobbish top ten?
At the rate they're going there will be no one
left for Virginia's birthday party...alive.

Happy Birthday to me X

COLUMBIA PICTURES PRESENTS
A JOHN DUNNING-ANDRÉ LINK PRODUCTION OF
A J. LEE THOMPSON FILM "HAPPY BIRTHDAY TO ME"
Starring MELISSA SUE ANDERSON · GLENN FORD · LAWRENCE DANE
SHARON ACKER · FRANCES HYLAND
Introducing TRACY BREGMAN and LISA LANGLOIS
Associate Producer LARRY NESIS Music by BO HARWOOD and LANCE RUBIN
Production Designer EARL PRESTON Director of Photography MIKLOS LENTE, C.S.C.
Screenplay by JOHN SAXTON, PETER JOBIN and TIMOTHY BOND
Story by JOHN SAXTON Line Producer STEWART HARDING
Produced by JOHN DUNNING and ANDRÉ LINK
Directed by J. LEE THOMPSON
Theme Song Sung by SYREETA Courtesy of Motown Records
Released by Columbia-EMI-Warner Distributors Ltd.

...ED TO THE PARTY.

was influenced by and even copied *Halloween*, as seen when the killer hides in the trees under the virginal Final Girl's window. The soundtrack – all tinkly electronic keyboards by Gary S. Scott – certainly goes beyond an homage to Carpenter's film. Unfortunately, the Final Girl (Cecile Bagdadi) – while likable enough – is no Jamie Lee Curtis. Further reducing the bare-bones approach of *Halloween*, the murderer here has no mask and seemingly no motive. Whether this is sheer laziness on the part of the filmmakers or a valid comment on the randomness of violence is left open to conjecture.

HELL NIGHT AND MORE

Linda Blair found notoriety as the world's most famous possessed child in *The Exorcist* (1973), and her genre career continued in 1981 when she took the lead in the enjoyably gothic-tinged *Hell Night*, in which horny teenagers spend the night in a supposedly haunted mansion with fatal results (see a full review on page 195).

Looking to get more mileage out of the slasher film, *Halloween*'s executive producer Irwin Yablan hoped lightning would strike twice. Director Tom DeSimone was well aware that the MPAA had come down hard on the film's contemporaries, so he de-emphasized gore for suspense. However, showing just how nervous filmmakers were becoming about that issue, the producers cut the film even before the censors had a chance to get their hands on it. Costing almost $1.5 million, *Hell Night* was a modest success at the box office when it opened in August 1981 with takings of $2.3 million.

The Unseen mixed murder, ex–Bond girl Barbara Bach and Danish folk music. Even more strange is the little-seen *A Day of Judgment*, which

Below British video cover for *Final Exam*.

Some may pass
the test...
God help the rest.

EMBASSY
Home Entertainment

FINAL EXAM

Right American
poster artwork for
Hell Night.

has the dubious distinction of being perhaps the first and probably last attempt to mix the slasher film and Christian morality play. A released mental patient goes on the rampage in Romano Scavolini's *Nightmare*. Undoubtedly one of the most graphically violent subgenre films from the early 1980s, its fearsome reputation was cemented when it became one of the most infamous of the British 'video nasties' under the title of *Nightmares in a Damaged Brain*.

HALLOWEEN II – MORE OF THE NIGHT HE CAME HOME

Perhaps, seeing the box-office returns, you would have thought a sequel to *Halloween* was a given, but back in 1981 the slasher sequel was still something of a novelty.

Donald Pleasence, speaking on the set of *Halloween 4: The Return of Michael Myers* (1988), told *Fangoria* that he had an inkling that there might be a direct sequel to the first film when they were filming the last sequence. John Carpenter had told him to take his gun and look out of the window: 'I said, "But John, there's nobody there." John

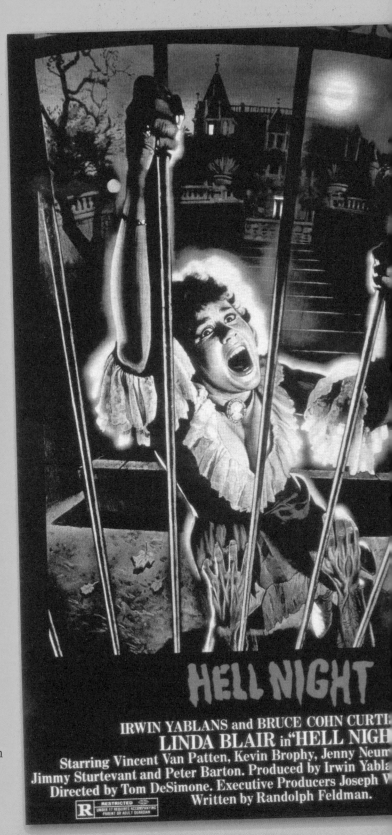

HELL NIGHT

IRWIN YABLANS and BRUCE COHN CURTI
LINDA BLAIR in "HELL NIGH
Starring Vincent Van Patten, Kevin Brophy, Jenny Neum
Jimmy Sturtevant and Peter Barton. Produced by Irwin Yabla
Directed by Tom DeSimone. Executive Producers Joseph V
Written by Randolph Feldman.

R RESTRICTED
UNDER 17 REQUIRES ACCOMPANYING
PARENT OR ADULT GUARDIAN

looked at me in an odd sort of way and said, "Would you believe *Halloween II*?"'

Perhaps understandably, John Carpenter was reluctant to return as director, fearing that he would get typecast. However, he was legally obliged to return in some capacity and agreed to write the screenplay – collaborating again with Debra Hill (who briefly toyed with the idea of directing). Carpenter struggled, as he felt there was nowhere to go with the story. To give it a twist, Carpenter decided to make Myers the brother of Laurie Strode – which unfortunately

single-handedly diluted the chilling randomness of the original. Other directors were considered – even David Lynch, according to the January issue of *Boxoffice* magazine – and they eventually settled on Rick Rosenthal, whose short *The Toyer* had impressed Carpenter.

Rosenthal was a big fan of the bloodless, suspense-driven *Halloween*, but Carpenter was aware that the horror landscape had changed by 1981. In the film, Jamie Lee Curtis finds a hospital to be no safe haven as Myers continues his dogged pursuit of her. Curtis originally wasn't keen to return either, as she had hoped to concentrate on

ブギーマン

誰・も・彼・を・殺・せ・な・

Above and right Japanese promotional artwork for *Halloween II*.

her nonhorror career. However, she was aware that she owed a lot to Carpenter and Hill – although she was ultimately disappointed that Laurie did not play a bigger role. But Curtis's role, or lack thereof, wasn't the problem – as Carpenter told the *Twilight Zone* magazine in 1982, the rough cut was 'as scary as Quincy', a reference to the the popular but gentle US TV series featuring a mild-mannered medical examiner turned sleuth.

Audiences demanded more visceral entertainment, and Rosenthal says Carpenter shot additional scenes to spice the film up and please the post–*Friday the 13th* crowd by adding more blood and guts. Despite its flaws, *Halloween II* works well as a straight slasher movie, with the nearly abandoned hospital a suitably creepy setting. It premiered on October 30, 1981, in 1,211 theatres, and audiences loved it. It had a final domestic take of over $25 million.

ON THE PROWL

Joseph Zito's *The Prowler* (originally announced under the title *Most Likely to Die*) was budgeted at around $1 million. Its central premise is remarkably similar to the same year's superior *My Bloody Valentine*; in both films, a killer's psychosis is retriggered by the reawakening of a long-dead tradition of a dance. A spurned GI kills his cheating sweetheart (the film was called *Rosemary's Killer* outside of the United States) in 1945 – in the present day the murders start again.

The film has good production values and some suspenseful chase sequences – and the killer's threatening army outfit is certainly memorable (shown to full effect on the poster artwork). However, like many of the slasher films released around the time, the real stars are the special effects, which are provided by Tom Savini. Throats are slashed, a woman is pitchforked in the shower and, in the most memorably nasty moment, a character has a knife thrust through the top of his head and out through his jaw (his eyeballs roll back into his head for that extra bit of Grand Guignol glee). The special effects were so realistic that people used to believe that Zito had actually killed people for real, much to his amusement. Given their starring role, it is somewhat ironic that these effects were invariably trimmed on the film's original release.

Sadly, the rest of the film isn't quite so arresting. *The Prowler* was nearly distributed by AVCO Embassy nationwide, but the deal fell through and it was distributed regionally – which probably affected its box office and its notoriety.

Shot in Utah in the summer of 1980, *Don't Go in the Woods* attempted to recreate

Below The Prowler comes calling.

Everyone has nightmares about the ugliest way to die.

DON'T GO IN THE WOODS ...alone!

R — WARNING CONTAINS SCENES OF GRAPHIC VIOLENCE

Starring **NICK McCLELLAND**

JAMES P. HAYDEN · KEN CARTER & TOM DRURY as The Monster

MANSON INTERNATIONAL

Copyright 1981 Double S Productions (Astral) Ltd. all rights reserved

VIDEO RELEASING ORGANIZATION

Above and right
British video artwork for *Don't Go in the Woods* and TV movie *Dark Night of the Scarecrow*.

some of that backwoods magic *of Friday the 13th*. Although the script for this infamously inept but perversely enjoyable effort supposedly preceded *Friday the 13th*, its influence is clear. Two couples on a camping trip are attacked by a psychotic mountain man.

The woods are also full of the kind of white trash that even Jerry Springer would baulk at having on his show – fat women huffing up hillsides, nerdy bird-watchers, roller-skating disco bunnies and swinging couples, all accompanied by perhaps the most grating score of all time (by H. Kingsley Thurber). At least the gore is plentiful, if extremely hokey. The film was fished from obscurity and ended up on the notorious 'video nasties' list under the title *Don't Go in the Woods . . . Alone!*

So successful was the subgenre in 1981 that the cinema market was arguably saturated by slashers – some great, many not. Its reach could even be felt on TV. In *Dark Night of the Scarecrow*, for example, a man with learning difficulties (Larry Drake) is wrongly accused of killing a young girl. He disguises himself as a scarecrow, but some local men find and kill him – only to find that they themselves are being stalked and killed by someone dressed in the very same costume. While the violence and sexual content were considerably toned down for the small screen, this minor classic is still a highly effective slice of the macabre with definite slasher movie leanings.

A terrifying suspense story

Dark Night

of the

SCARECROW

1982 – CAMP AND CREEPY

The slasher movie peaked by 1982 and began its slow descent towards straight-to-video hell. However, there was still blood to be rung from the subgenre yet, as the supernatural began to feature more heavily and a certain psycho put on his iconic hockey mask for the first time.

Below American poster artwork for *Madman*.

They thought they were alone.

One of the first slasher movies released in 1982 was Joe Giannone's *Madman*. Alternatively cheap and cheerful, and sometimes even a little creepy, it was a late arrival in the already crowded summer-camp-slaughter cycle. A big-mouthed teenager rouses a local legend – the psychotic, hulking farmer Madman Marz – who proceeds to hack up counsellors one by one. Like *The Burning*, *Madman* was based on the urban Cropsy Maniac legend from New York State. In fact, although the film got the go-ahead in August 1980, news of *The Burning* put the production on hold as they assessed if the world could handle two Cropsys. After the plot was reworked, *Madman* was shot on Long Island in late 1980. Despite some of the cheesiest performances ever committed to celluloid, it manages some fairly suspenseful sequences, particularly when one of the counsellors chooses to hide inside a fridge. *Madman* made the top 10 *Variety* list the week of its New York opening and did especially well on video.

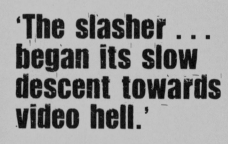

'The slasher . . . began its slow descent towards video hell.'

THE LAW OF DIMINISHING RETURNS

The Seduction was written and directed by David Schmoeller. Unfortunately, this dire attempt to add an erotic edge to the slasher showed little of the promise he hinted at in his earlier and far superior film *Tourist Trap*. The film's producers insisted on casting Morgan Fairchild, and she spends

most of the film nearly nude while contending with a crazed stalker (Andrew Stevens). *Halloween* executive producer Irwin Yablans, who also produced this film, may have found that the law of diminishing returns rang all too true with *The Seduction* in regards to suspense. But it proved a hit, earning $11 million at the box office. It also preceded the erotic thrillers that proliferated in early 1990s cinema. Despite its financial success, critics hated it, and even Schmoeller later stated that the film was an embarrassment.

Perhaps in a move that showed that the slasher movie's influence was spreading (or more likely smacked of producer's desperation to find ways to keep box-office cash registers opening), *Silent Rage* attempted to mix martial arts with stalk 'n' slash. Chuck Norris battles a psychotic killer, who is accidentally given superhuman powers when a trial drug is tested on him. Silly but undeniably fun, *Silent Rage* did well at the domestic box office, taking in around $10 million.

The fertile slasher setting of the hospital was given another outing in the aftermath of the financial success of *Halloween II* with the glossy Canadian production *Visiting Hours* (originally named *The Fright*). Despite high-production values, it was something of a return to the hard-edged thrills of earlier slashers. Michael Ironside acts in a scarily effective role as a woman-hating psychopath pursuing a feminist

Left and below
American poster artwork for *The Seduction* and *Silent Rage.*

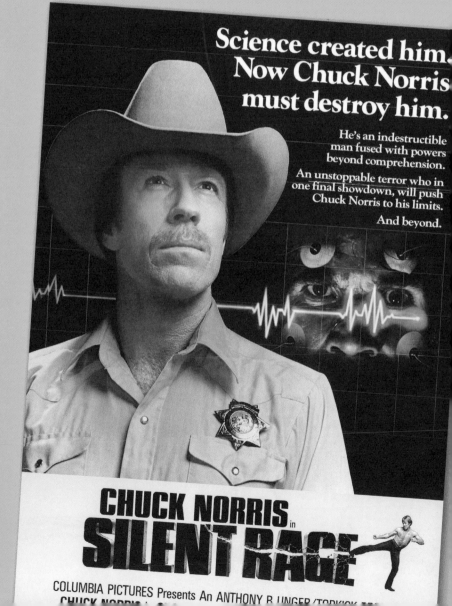

Below and right
American poster
artwork for *Visiting
Hours* and *Pranks*.

TV journalist, played by Lee Grant, as she recuperates in hospital. On the surface *Visiting Hours* appears to be a more conventional thriller, with the atypically middle-aged Grant as the heroine and Final Girl. However, it is a slasher flick through and through, playing on a common fear (this time of hospitals) and featuring cat-and-mouse antics between the chaser and chased. It is also interesting because it pits liberal feminism against macho right-wing bigotry – a battle that was happening for real in America at the time.

The theme of what happens when a pacifist has to resort to aggressive violence to survive is a familiar one in the slasher, but it is done successfully here. Distributed by Fox, *Visiting Hours* was a sizable hit, scoring over $13 million at the box office before falling victim to the video crackdown in Britain, becoming yet another 'video nasty'. Also released the same year, *X-Ray* had a hospital setting too but was a cheesier proposition.

Sporting a soundtrack akin to putting the music of *Psycho* and *Friday the 13th* in a blender (the surprising

"The Villain
Makes
Coed Stew."
—*Bill Cosford, Miami Herald*

PRANKS

A JEFF OBROW PRODUCTION "PRANKS" Starring LAURIE LAPINSKI • STEPHEN SACHS
Associate Producer STACEY GIACHINO • Music By CHRIS YOUNG
Screenplay By STEPHEN CARPENTER • JEFFREY OBROW • STACEY GIACHINO
Production Consultant ROBERT L. NEWMAN • Production Associates SAMSON ASLANIAN • JOHN HOPKINS
Produced By JEFFREY OBROW • Directed By JEFFREY OBROW • STEPHEN CARPENTER
Color By GETTY FILM LABORATORY • Distributed by NEW IMAGE RELEASING, INC. In Association With WESCOM
© 1982 NEW IMAGE RELEASING, INC., ALL RIGHTS RESERVED

début of Hollywood composer Christopher Young), *The Dorm That Dripped Blood* (originally released in 1982 as *Pranks*) was made for just $90,000. It features a group of strangely mature-looking students who stay behind to close down a dorm during the holidays, only to be bumped off, one by one, by a mysterious assailant. The result of a collaboration between UCLA graduates Stephen Carpenter and Jeffrey Obrow, this was yet another slasher branded a 'video nasty' in the United Kingdom (see its feature spread on page 126).

Honeymoon Horror takes place on an island, with the machete- and axe-wielding killer a close cousin of Cropsy over at Camp Blackwood. Made in Texas for the

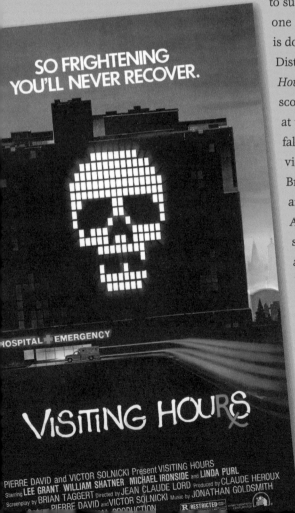

SO FRIGHTENING
YOU'LL NEVER RECOVER.

HOSPITAL ✚ EMERGENCY

VISITING HOURS

PIERRE DAVID and VICTOR SOLNICKI Present VISITING HOURS
Starring LEE GRANT WILLIAM SHATNER MICHAEL IRONSIDE and LINDA PURL Produced by CLAUDE HEROUX
Screenplay by BRIAN TAGGERT Directed by JEAN CLAUDE LORD Music by JONATHAN GOLDSMITH
PIERRE DAVID and VICTOR SOLNICKI **R** RESTRICTED

threadbare sum of $50,000, this dog-eared production has a hideously burnt maniac hacking up newlyweds and coeds in tight shorts. It was one of the first slashers to find its main audience on video – some unverified reports say that it made Sony $22 million in rentals alone on the then-fledgling medium.

Despite budgets getting smaller and story lines sillier, the slasher movie still showed it could surprise. *Alone in the Dark* has not one but several mental patients escaping from an asylum and is a deliciously bitter cocktail of jet-black humour, thrills, spills and terror. Donald Pleasence – borrowing from his Dr. Loomis character in *Halloween* – stars as a well-meaning but decidedly off-the-wall psychiatrist. He is joined in the film by genre veterans Martin Landau and Jack Palance. Showing that the subgenre was already self-consciously parodying itself by 1982, *Alone in the Dark* is darkly

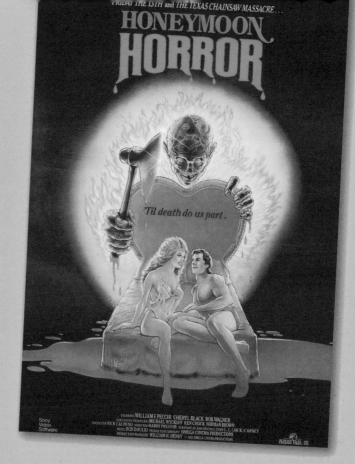

humorous without tipping into farce. In a very nice touch, the escapees find that the outside world is even more dysfunctional than the asylum, as they stumble across a riot during a power cut. The most infamous image from the film is that of a knife shooting up through a mattress between the legs of a babysitter, and although the phallic implications there are clear, it is fair to say that the majority of the violence is committed by men against other men.

Directed by Jack Sholder – the editor of *The Burning* – *Alone in the Dark* was budgeted to cost around $1 million. Despite Tom Savini providing one of the film's shock effects, it ultimately proved too

Above and left American poster artwork for *Honeymoon Horror*, and another crispy villain in the same low-budget movie (*left*).

Below Japanese promotional flyer for *Alone in the Dark*.

cerebral for audiences expecting another *Friday the 13th* (something that would shortly be available to them).

FRANCHISES – *FRIDAY THE 13TH PART 3*

The most successful slasher film of 1982, *Friday the 13th Part 3* grossed a massive $36 million domestically. In the first three days of release alone, it grossed something

ALONE
IN
THE
DARK

'Give me something to scream about.'

– Chili, *Friday the 13th Part 3*

over $9 million, beating the same weekend total of Spielberg's *E.T.*, that summer's box-office champ. Going against the law of diminishing returns, it bucked the trend by making $14 million more than *Part 2* in 1981. Director Steve Miner returned and the plot was more of the same but had cosmetic changes, such as replacing camp counsellors with teenage vacationers. Dana Kimmell led the doomed youngsters as Chris, who had previously tussled with Jason Voorhees and lived to tell the tale. *Part 3* was very successful in its use of 3D; the move into the third dimension no doubt helped its box-office success.

The film is topped off by Kimmell succumbing to a fit of bad acting as she is driven away by the authorities after being attacked by Mrs. Voorhees, who seems to have recovered from her decapitation in the first film. An alternative ending, in which Jason whacks off Chris's head with a machete, was seemingly shot but has yet to surface. *Friday the 13th Part 3* is still very entertaining, although it is a perfect example of how, by 1982, the slasher was taking itself increasingly less seriously and was content to veer closer to camp.

A DEMON TOO FAR

Canadian body-horror specialist David
Cronenberg (perhaps most famous for
the 1981 film *Scanners* and the remake of
The Fly in 1986) passed on the directorial
duties when he was offered the job of
bringing author Ray Russell's *The Incubus*
to the screen. The story of a demon with a
massive penis stalking a small town might
seem designed to appeal to him; however,
even in the progressive early 1980s North
American cinema, this detail would have
been too much for audiences – even
though, in the finished film, the rapes and
murders are still mostly implied rather
than on-screen. However, it finishes with a

climactic twist that manages to go beyond
nightmarish into genuinely unhinged. It
also performed respectably at the domestic
box office, taking $13,110,874.

A strikingly different take on the genre
is J. S. Cardone's film *The Slayer*. Although
it all but evaporated on its release near
the end of 1982, it is likely that it was
a major influence on one of the most
successful slasher franchises of all time.
Unlike most of the competition, it is
defiantly teen free and has a genuinely
unnerving atmosphere, featuring a woman
who becomes increasingly disturbed after
continuing to be plagued by nightmares of
a supernatural bogeyman. Soon, the line

Above Dana Kimmell
finds out the perils
of being a Final
Girl when she's
menaced by Jason
Voorhees in *Friday
the 13th Part 3*.

Below and right
Mexican poster
artwork for *The
Incubus* and the
British video cover
for *The Slayer*.

between reality and nightmare becomes blurred, as people begin to meet horrible deaths. This should sound familiar: it is eerily similar to Wes Craven's wildly successful *A Nightmare on Elm Street*, which was released several years after this film. *The Slayer* found itself yet another victim of the 'video nasties' hysteria.

Also trying to mix the supernatural with slasher movie theatrics was James W. Roberson's entertaining *Superstition*. Perhaps not a slasher in the strictest sense, it does apply the body-count approach to teenage victims with admirable low-budget gusto. The supernatural angle – with the vengeful spirit of a witch that takes revenge on a new priest and his family – also allowed the filmmakers creative kill license. *Superstition* was tremendously popular in Britain – so much so, that it was one of the few films to get a subsequent cinema release as *The Witch* in 1984, several years after enjoying great success on video under its better-known title. *Superstition* escaped the 'nasties' hysteria,

unlike the mostly tedious *Unhinged*, which is punctuated by a few flashes of graphic violence (courtesy of a scythe-wielding maniac). The amateurish and thoroughly woeful *Whodunit?* escaped, too, but it showed that even a slasher this hopeless would be released theatrically in an effort to turn a profit on a small budget.

L. Scott Castillo Jr.'s *Satan's Blade*, made during 1980 and 1981, is another attempt to mix the supernatural with more traditional knife play. Here, a group of female bank robbers and tourists are attacked by the 'blade' during a snowy winter getaway at a remote lodge. The film's troubled shoot was hampered by the inexperienced director and his insistence on shooting on

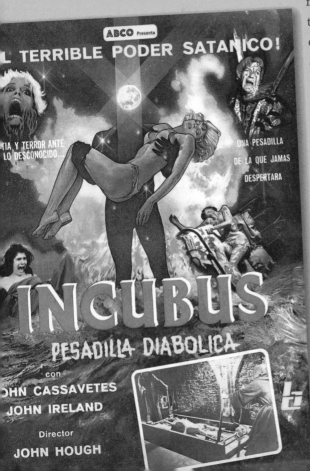

is it a nightmare...
or is it . . .

The Slayer

Starring **Sarah Kendall, Fredrick J. Flynn, Carol Kottenbrook, Alan McRae**
Directed by **J. S. Cardone** Produced by **William R. Ewing**
Executive Producer **Lloyd N. Adams**
SEE WARNING ON REVERSE

RUNNING TIME 89 MINS APPROX.

VIPCO

ABCO Presenta

L TERRIBLE PODER SATANICO!

TIA Y TERROR ANTE
LO DESCONOCIDO...

UNA PESADILLA
DE LA QUE JAMAS
DESPERTARA

INCUBUS
PESADILLA DIABOLICA

con
OHN CASSAVETES
JOHN IRELAND

Director
JOHN HOUGH

¡Los que murieron

fueron más afortunad

VTC

VTC 1036
Distributed by

HORROR

Superstition

You'll believe it
just before
you die...

Superstición

Above and right
Mexican lobby card
for *Superstition* and
the British video
artwork for the same
title (*right*).

THE RISE AND FALL OF THE 'NASTIES'

'Video nasty' was the British tabloid term invented in the early 1980s for the type of violent horror and exploitation movies especially popular at the time. A sizable number were slashers, including *The Burning*, *Bloody Moon* (see Mexican artwork at right), *Don't Go in the House* and *Pranks* (see British video artwork below). In the early 1980s, the British video market was flooded with hundreds of previously unseen, unedited and uncensored films, due to a loophole in the law. Public hysteria, whipped up by sensational newspaper headlines and campaigning by politicians and religious groups, created what can only be described as a witch hunt on horror movies, which were blamed for everything from juvenile delinquency to the collapse of society itself.

The infamous Director of Public Prosecutions (DPP) list of films liable for prosecution under the Obscene Publications Act first appeared in June 1983. Shelves were cleared in video stores across Britain by zealous police forces, and 39 films were effectively banned as a result of prosecution under the law. Ironically, a number of films that had been given a cinema certificate by the BBFC were also targeted by this new moral fervour. Slashers as relatively innocuous as *The Funhouse* also found themselves under scrutiny.

The Video Recordings Act of 1984 was hurriedly assembled, ensuring that all videos released in Britain would be previewed and censored by the BBFC. The legacy of the hysteria of the previous years meant that many slashers were subsequently heavily cut or had their releases on video delayed; some, such as the *Friday the 13th* franchise, were delayed by several years, with a cut version of *Part 3* only appearing on video in the United Kingdom in 1987.

In recent years, the more relaxed attitude towards film censorship in Britain has meant that many former 'video nasty' slashers have received uncut releases to DVD. Indeed, with lip-smacking irony, most wear their badge of former notoriety with honour to sell themselves to fresh and unwitting blood-thirsty audiences.

When the kidding stops ...the killing starts!

PRANKS

Left and below
British and
American video
artwork for
Satan's Blade.

MOGUL

35 mm, an extravagance for a low-budget slasher. Despite postproduction in 1982, the film was barely released. Prism Films rescued it from complete obscurity two years later when it was put out on video in the United States.

Many slashers were made but not released until several years later. For example, there is a trailer for *The Scaremaker* that suggests that it got a release in 1982 through Aries International and Independent International, but it sat on the shelf for two years before its release as *Girls Nite Out*. This tale of murder during a college scavenger hunt features a murderer dressed in a bear costume

SATANS BLADE

Below American poster artwork for *Girls Nite Out*.

Far right American poster artwork for *The Slumber Party Massacre*.

with knives as his fingers (anticipating Freddy Krueger once again). It has a strongly misogynistic edge, featuring insults such as 'Slut! Bitch! Whore!' which are hissed as the coeds are killed. It doesn't have a Final Girl, in contrast to other slashers of the time. However, the film's closing moments resonate with a scene of genuine creepiness that is missing from the rest of the film.

Hoping to score a slice of the box office that *Halloween II* had scared up the previous year, the execrable *Trick or Treats* demonstrated just how quickly the quality of the subgenre was slipping. This film also showed that filmmakers were still ripping off Carpenter's movie a good four years after its original release – in this case, the babysitter is stalked by someone who has escaped from an asylum.

FEMINIST SLASHER?

The Slumber Party Massacre was atypical in many senses – and almost seemed a pastiche of the slasher. The viewer sees a group of high school girls blissfully unaware that a psycho with a portable power drill has escaped from an asylum and is about to return to town to torment them. Perhaps most interestingly, it was directed by a woman (Amy Holden Jones), and the script was written by a bisexual feminist activist (Rita Mae Brown).

Because the film was in production at the very height of protests about violence against women in cinema, it is tempting to see it as a kind of crypto-feminist slasher flick. Certainly the implications are clear when we see the symbolic emasculation of the killer, when a girl fights back and manages to snap his intentionally phallic drill bit in half, but women fighting back in horror flicks was certainly nothing new – and, if anything, post-*Halloween*, it was almost de rigueur.

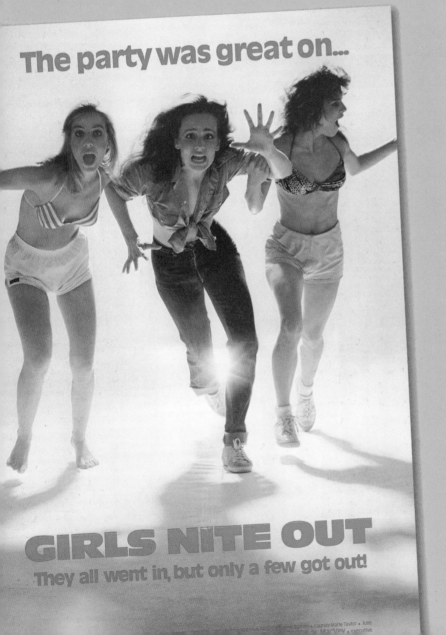

The party was great on...

GIRLS NITE OUT

They all went in, but only a few got out!

Perhaps ironically, the film does feature an almost unprecedented amount of naked female flesh, but Jones maintains that legendary film producer and financier of the film Roger Corman insisted that she film those scenes against her wishes. As far as the violence goes, Jones racks it up against the male characters; out of about nine bodies, six are men. 'Maybe I was getting back at all the obnoxious teenage boys I knew', she said. Be it straight exploitation, a generic slasher flick or a satirical take on the subgenre, many feminists clearly didn't get the joke.

BIG TROUBLE

Humongous was director Paul Lynch's second foray into slasherdom. His *Prom Night* follow-up tale of teenagers shipwrecked on Dog Island, where a barking killer resides, is certainly not designed to be taken that seriously either. The victims-to-be snarl, pout and wear disco headbands. Most of them have the charisma of plywood, but at least there is the guilty pleasure of watching them die. There is also a scene when one girl collects berries in her cleavage, which is certainly novel. *Humongous* is hampered by an overly dark picture, which makes it difficult to see what's going on most of the time. Unfortunately, when you do see him, the killer has a face that looks like a giant baked potato with a boiled egg balanced

Close your eyes for a second...and sleep forever

The SLUMBER PARTY MASSACRE

Starring MICHELE MICHAELS · ROBIN STILLE · MICHAEL VILLELA
ANDRE HONORE · Screenplay by RITA MAE BROWN
Produced and Directed by AMY JONES
© 1982 Santa Fe Productions, Inc.

Below and far right
British video cover
for *The Last Horror
Film* and Mexican
lobby card for *Blood
Song* (*right*).

carefully on top. A change at the top of AVCO Embassy ensured that it was barely released to theatres.

A PLACE FOR IDOLS TO GO

Perhaps one of the strangest pieces of casting in slasher movie history was singer and former 1950s teen idol Frankie Avalon as a psychotic killer in *Blood Song*. Only four years previously he had serenaded high school students in *Grease* – but now he had graduated to butchering them with a hatchet. Stretching credulity even further, Avalon is a flute-playing escapee from an asylum, who appears to have developed a psychic link with a crippled teenage girl (Donna Wilkes) after a blood transfusion. In a trance, she witnesses his killing spree in what is perhaps one of the most bizarre of all slashers. It ends with Avalon chewing scenery with gusto while chasing Wilkes in a forklift around a warehouse, screaming 'I really like you, Marion!'

English director David Winters hoped to recreate the financial success of William Lustig's *Maniac*, when he cast the film's star in *The Last Horror Film*. Joe Spinell – so sweatily effective in his earlier role – plays the number-one fan of a scream queen (Caroline Munro), whose entourage is being gorily offed by a mysterious killer. Whereas *Maniac* was unremittingly grim, *The Last Horror Film* is pure camp. Despite its self-reflective nature, the film failed to find an audience on large screen in theatres but did eventually find one on video.

Rounding out 1982, *Too Scared to Scream* saw murders at an upscale apartment complex, while the bizarre Wisconsin-filmed *Blood Beat* seemed to have a seven-foot-tall samurai conjured up by female masturbation. Made in 1978, the loopy axe-murder opus *Dark Sanity* got a belated release, and the mildly diverting *Death Valley* distinguished itself by having a young boy dodging the attentions of a psychotic killer.

alpha video

JOE SPINELL & CAROLINE MUNRO IN

THE *LAST* HORROR FILM

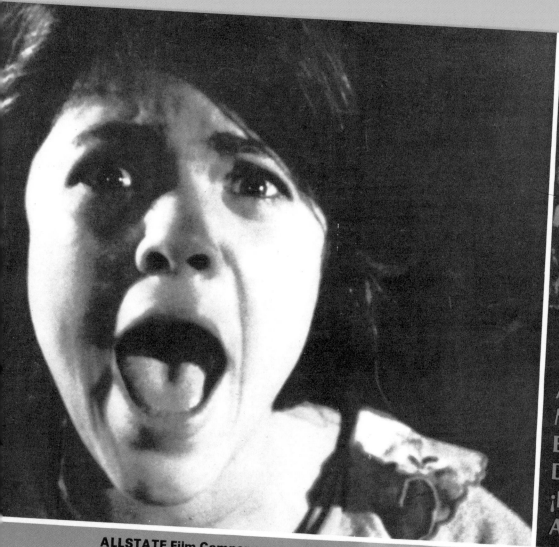

AQUELLA
MUSICA
ERA PRELUDIO
DE MUERTE...
¡DE UN SICOPATA
ASESINO!

ALLSTATE Film Company presenta a:

KIE AVALON   DONNA WILKES   DANE CLARK
en

LODIA SINIESTRA

(Blood Song)

ALAN J. LEVI   Productores: FRANK AVIANCA y LEE SHROUT   en COLOR
ES FARGO, FRANK AVIANCA y LENNY MONTANA   Música: MONTY TURNER

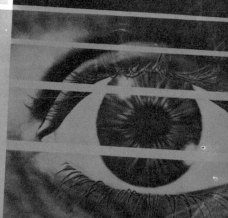

1983 — A COUPLE OF TWISTS

By 1983 the Golden Age of the slasher movie was fast coming to a close. What had been cutting-edge terror only a few years previously was now looking decidedly old hat.

Below and far right American poster artwork for *The House on Sorority Row* and British video artwork for *Double Exposure* (*right*).

Even the emerging franchises took the year off, with no *Friday the 13th* movie and the *Halloween* series having dumped the slasher angle with the Michael Myers–less *Halloween III: Season of the Witch* in the previous year. Still, the low budgets and potentially high profits meant that there were still those willing to risk new enterprises or simply foolhardy enough to dust off those half-remembered productions that were sitting on the shelf.

A FEW NEW TRICKS IN THE OLD DOG YET?

Even by this late stage there were still some tricks left to play. In early 1983, one of the best slasher movies of the period was released. Mark Rosman managed to make an exciting, suspenseful and stylish film with *The House on Sorority Row*. To give the film a twist, Rosman wanted to kill off his Final Girl and shot an ending where she was found floating face down in a swimming pool. However, the film's distributor had other ideas and insisted on a more ambiguous close (see review on page 196). Despite flawed poster artwork that made it look like a soft-core porn movie, *The House on Sorority Row* bucked the trend and

'It is a heady concoction of incest and homophobia.'

made a tidy profit of over $10 million at the domestic box office.

Double Exposure, on the other hand, was something of an ego trip for lead actor and producer Michael Callan. He plays a middle-aged photographer who is seemingly irresistible to women. The one problem is that he dreams he is killing his models – and when he wakes they really are dead. Unusually complex and

NOTHING CAN PREPARE YOU FOR WHAT HAPPENS WHEN SHE FIGHTS BACK.

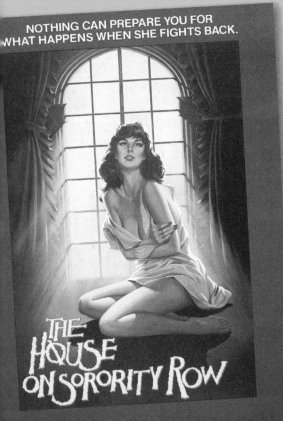

THE HOUSE ON SORORITY ROW

WHERE NOTHING IS OFF LIMITS

EDWARD L. MONTORO presents a MARK ROSMAN Film
THE HOUSE ON SORORITY ROW starring KATHRYN McNEIL HELEN DAVIDSON
Music by RICHARD H. BAND Executive Producers JOHN PONCHOCK and W. THOMAS McMAHON
Produced by MARK ROSMAN and JOHN G. CLARK Written and Directed by MARK ROSMAN

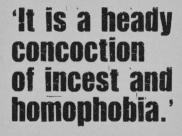

multilayered, *Double Exposure* is still primarily an exercise in exploitation. There are acres of naked female flesh and gimmicky murders aplenty. In an attempt to feature too many twists and turns, the film ultimately becomes muddled and trips over its own contrivances.

Director William Asher's *Night Warning* is another interestingly atypical subgenre film; it gained a certain amount of notoriety when it was released on video in the United Kingdom under the title *Nightmare Maker* and was subsequently banned. Made in 1981, it is a heady concoction that includes incest and homophobia, combined with a classic Oedipus tale. Susan Tyrrell gives a strikingly demented performance as a middle-aged woman who will kill to keep her teenage nephew from leaving home. Like Baby Jane Hudson's younger sister in the iconic *What Ever Happened to Baby Jane?* (1962), she portrays a woman deep in psychosis who can still maintain a faltering mask of normality. Lips drawn back in a lopsided sneer, clutching a machete and chasing a

DOUBLE EXPOSURE

Starring
MICHAEL CALLAN,
JOANNA PETTET,
JAMES STACY

18

SMILE AND SAY "DIE!"

Below and far right
British video artwork
for *Nightmare Maker*
and a reflective
scene in this
Mexican lobby card
for *Curtains* (right).

poor unfortunate soul through a stormy night – the sight of Tyrrell is unforgettable.

Another film, which sat on the shelf before a belated release, was the Canadian production *Curtains*. Producer Peter Simpson hit box-office gold in 1980 with

Prom Night, and he was keen to rush another slasher into production. Originally a supernatural-edged 'slice 'em, dice 'em' film, *Curtains* was billed as the 'ultimate nightmare' – and, from the sound of it, for the filmmakers at least, it was. Partially shot in 1980 – and then on and off over the next two years – it sat until 1983. One actress was fired for not being able to act, and the director took his name off the project after Simpson ordered two weeks of reshoots. Whole scenes vanished, never to be seen again. However, that's not to say that this tale of actresses battling for the part of a lifetime, at a remote snowbound mansion, is without interest. Visually, it is rich and quirky – many scenes open with the theatrical swish of a black curtain. *Curtains* also features one of the most stylish chase sequences in the history of the slasher, during which subgenre regular Lesleh Donaldson is pursued across a frozen lake in slow motion by an ice-skating assassin wearing a hag mask and holding a scythe. Unfortunately, as a whole, *Curtains* comes across like *A Chorus Line* meets *Friday the 13th*.

MIXING GENRES

J. Lee Thompson – the director of *Happy Birthday to Me* – made a lesser return to the subgenre with *10 to Midnight*, starring Charles Bronson. In the same way that *Silent Rage* had attempted to mix the subgenre with martial arts, Thompson tried to mix it with the right-wing vigilantism sub-subgenre that Bronson had already

ATLANTIS

She was lonely
He was all she had
No-one would take him from her —
and live.....

Named Best Horror Film
of 1982 by the Academy
of Science Fiction,
Fantasy, and Horror.

NIGHTMARE MAKER

SEPULCROS
LA ULTIMA LLAMADA

6 Jovenes y bellas
artistas y un
maniatico director
que maneja el terror
y los entierros

con JOHN VERNON SAMANTA EGGAR

Below British video artwork for *The Final Terror*.

If you go down to the woods today you're sure of...

THORN EMI

766

THE FINAL TERROR (18)

starring
DARRYL HANNAH
RACHEL WARD

made all his own. The film's tag line is even designed to inflame: 'Forget what's legal . . . do what's right'. Bronson spends as much time battling liberals as he does the naked killer (Gene Davis), whose underpants stay on in the TV version. The film also recalls the real-life murders of Richard Speck when Davis, clutching a knife, invades the apartment of four student nurses. The movie was a modest success at the box office.

The Final Terror juxtaposes urban teenagers with a primal terror – actually an insane woman who has become feral. She is shown camouflaged by her surroundings, covered in moss and leaves. Curiously muted but similar to many of the backwoods slashers from this time, the film features happy campers roasting marshmallows and telling creepy stories around the campfire. If it all seemed curiously dated by 1983, that was because it was made in 1981 – the height of the slasher craze. It eventually saw the light of day due to the subsequent popularity of its young cast. Daryl Hannah was on the verge of the big time with *Splash* (1984) and Rachel Ward – already a slasher movie veteran of *Night School* – was starring in the popular TV adaptation of *The Thorn Birds*. During the film's theatrical release, at least one cinema in Charlotte, North Carolina, joined forces with a camping store to put a themed display in the lobby. It is not known whether the sales of camping goods spiked or, indeed, helped *The Final Terror* bring in cinema goers.

PSYCHO II

Making a sequel to Hitchcock's *Psycho* (see page 29) was ambitious, but near the end of the 1980s slasher movie boom, that is

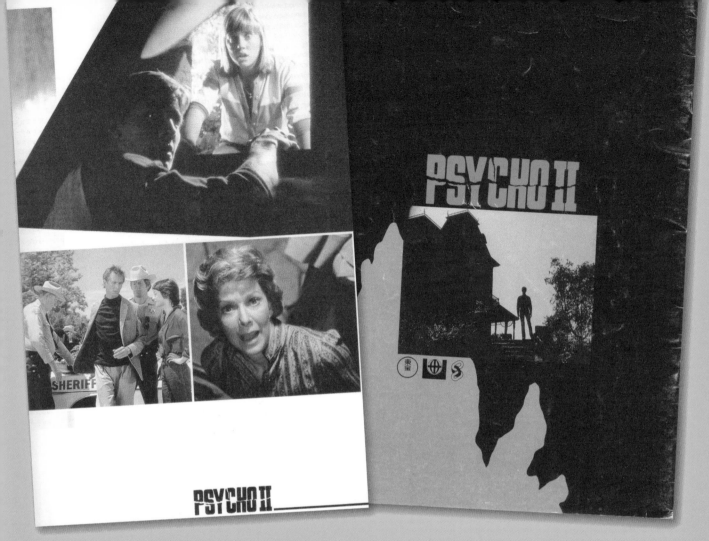

PSYCHO II

Above **Japanese promotional artwork for *Psycho II*.**

exactly what director Richard Franklin and writer Tom Holland did. *Psycho II* opens with a recap of the *Psycho*'s famous shower scene. While it invites unfavourable comparisons with the original, at least it tackles its formidable legacy head on.

Norman Bates (Anthony Perkins, reprising his famous role) is judged restored to sanity and free to leave custody, despite the protests of Lila Loomis (Vera Miles, also reprising her earlier role as the sister of Janet Leigh's character). Bates spends much of the film hesitating over

knives like an alcoholic craving a glass of scotch. The film uses familiar themes, both visual and thematic, from the original – showers, peep holes in the bathroom wall and naked female bodies. Franklin plays lip service to the contemporary subgenre with the introduction of horny, pot-smoking 1980s teen victims and fairly graphic slasher murders. Supposedly, Jamie Lee Curtis was considered for Tilly's role – which would have provided perfect symmetry, seeing as John Carpenter is said to have hired her for *Halloween*

Right and far right
American poster
artwork for *Pieces*
and British video art
for *Mortuary*.

'I do have affection for Norman as a person. . . . He is, at heart, a benevolent soul, with a dark side.'

– Anthony Perkins on Norman Bates

because of her mother's role in Hitchcock's original. Curtis, of course, was in Franklin's earlier quasi slasher, *Road Games* (1981).

Suspenseful and craftily plotted, *Psycho II* is perhaps better than it has any right to be. Not surprisingly, the film met with mixed reviews but scared up an impressive $34,725,000 at the domestic box office – a lot more than most slasher movies of the time. It was subsequently followed by the Perkins-helmed *Psycho III* (1986) and *Psycho IV: The Beginning* (1990).

Mortuary had been in preproduction as far back as 1980 but did not get a US release until September 1983. A teenager – Mary Beth McDonough from TV's wholesome *The Waltons* – finds it hard to come to terms with her father's death. She is pursued by a stranger in a black cape clutching an embalming pipe. *Mortuary* features a lengthy roller-boogie scene and Bill Paxton (who also appeared in the TV slasher *Deadly Lessons* in 1983 and would soon find fame in 1984's *The Terminator*) as a terminally goofy teen. The film's

YOU DON'T HAVE T
FOR A CHAINSAW

ABSOLUTELY NO ONE
UNDER 17 ADMITTED
TO THIS PERFORMANCE

PIEC

IT'S EXACTLY WHAT YOU

Starring **CHRISTOPHER GEORGE**
EDMUND PURDOM LINDA DAY
Screenplay by **DICK RANDALL & JOH**
Produced by **DICK RANDALL & STEVE MANASI**

YOUR F...
BEFORE
YOU ARE BURIED...

BEFORE
YOU ARE COVERED
WITH THE LAST
SHOVELFUL OF DIRT...

BE SURE YOU ARE
REALLY DEAD!

MORTUARY

...WHERE NOBODY RESTS IN PEACE

SLASHER SPOOFS (1978–84)

Horror spoofs were nothing new, as anyone who has seen an Abbott and Costello film (such as *Hold That Ghost*, 1941) will tell you. Many films – including the 'old dark house' chillers from the 1930s (see page 21) – attempted to balance horror with humour. However, the pattern for modern slasher spoofs was set after the release of *Psycho*. The shower scene from the film has become so iconic that it has been spoofed in a number of other movies.

The release of both *Halloween* and *Friday the 13th* started a new run of spoofs of the subgenre in the early 1980s. Of course, when a popular genre is spoofed, it is usually a sign that the cycle is coming to an end – and that was certainly true of the slasher boom in the 1980s. How could audiences continue to be terrified by plot devices and well-worn clichés when they were mercilessly dissected and played for laughs in other contemporary films? It is a testament to the popularity of the slasher that it periodically bounces back into favour.

Student Bodies (1981) was released during the height of popularity of the subgenre and was the first out-and-out spoof (see American poster artwork at right). It shows a house just like the one in *Halloween*; during a time lapse, it goes from *'Halloween'* to *'Friday the 13th'* to *'Jamie Lee Curtis's birthday.'* It features a killer called 'The Breather' who

keeps on stepping in chewing gum as the camera focuses on his boots. He murders girls with everything from a paper clip to an eggplant and suffocates boys with garbage bags. There is also an on-screen body counter.

Directed by Alfred Sole – who made the excellent proto-slasher *Communion* in 1976 – *Pandemonium* (1982) is set at a cheerleading academy, at which several teenagers had previously been murdered with a javelin. (See

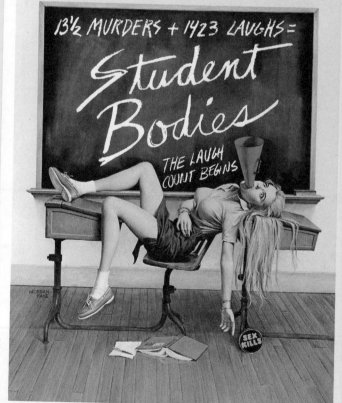

AT LAST
THE WORLD'S FIRST
COMEDY HORROR MOVIE.

13½ MURDERS + 1423 LAUGHS =

Student Bodies

THE LAUGH COUNT BEGINS

SEX KILLS

PARAMOUNT PICTURES PRESENTS "STUDENT BODIES" STARRING KRISTEN RITER, MATT GOLDSBY, RICHARD BRANDO as The Breather EXECUTIVE PRODUCERS JERRY BELSON

**Finally,
movie that is totally
taste-free.**

PANDEMONIUM

A KROST / CHAPIN PRODUCTION

...ANE TOM SMOTHERS in "PANDEMONIUM" with DEBRALEE SCOTT and CANDY AZZARA
...ecutive Producer BARRY KROST Written by RICHARD WHITLEY and JAIME KLEIN
Produced by DOUG CHAPIN Directed by ALFRED SOLE TECHNICOLOR® PANAVISION® United Artists

From United Artists Corporation

audience in the States and, rightly or wrongly, presumed that they would rather see American teenagers sliced and diced).

The National Lampoon crew turned their attention to spoofing the slasher with the woeful *Class Reunion* in 1982. *Wacko* was filmed in 1981 but not released until 1983. George Kennedy (from *Just before Dawn*) leads the cast against a pumpkin-headed serial killer who chases students on a lawnmower. With such characters as 'The Looney' and 'The Weirdo', the film is anything but subtle.

The subgenre continued to get spoofed in everything from *Killer Party* (1986), *Return to Horror High* (1987) and John Waters's *Serial Mom* (1994). However, the slasher really hit pay dirt with the phenomenally successful *Scary Movie* franchise (which started in 2000 and launched off the success of *Scream* and *I Know What You Did Last Summer*). Despite its shortcomings, it was one of the few spoofs that made more money at the box office than the films it was satirizing.

above for British video artwork). Almost 20 years later, a once-rejected cheerleader named Bambi reopens the academy. The film, which has a relatively star-studded cast, including Paul Reubens (who went on to fame as Pee Wee Herman) and Carol Kane (who appeared in *When a Stranger Calls*), is silly but amusing. A clever touch is the Canadian Mountie investigating the murders in an American town – a nod to Canadian slashers, such as *My Bloody Valentine*, which passed themselves off as American to audiences (a common occurrence during the Golden Age, as filmmakers saw their biggest potential

**WACKO...
the comedy
that takes off
where airplane landed**

WACKO

Starring
JOE DON BAKER STELLA STEVENS
GEORGE KENNEDY

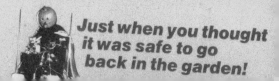

*Just when you thought
it was safe to go
back in the garden!*

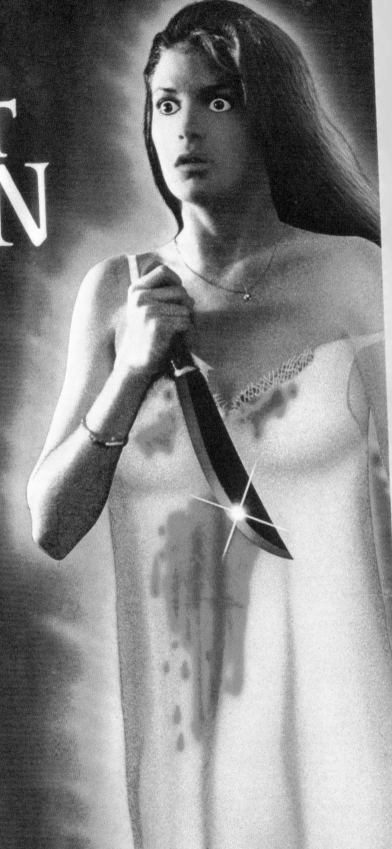

poster – showing a hand bursting out from a grave – has nothing to do with what is in the film but hints that the distributors were aware of the fading box-office draw of the slasher and were trying to hoodwink audiences into thinking they were going to see something else entirely.

'Melissa is a big hit with the local boys.'

Lynda Day George also starred in *Mortuary* but had a bigger role as a policewoman who poses as a tennis ace in *Pieces*. Promising that you didn't have to go to Texas for a chainsaw massacre, this cheerful tale of bodily dismemberment at a Boston college has built up a reputation over the years as one of the worst – but, paradoxically if you like bad movies, best – early 1980s slashers. It is not hard to see why. Blessed with half-decent production values, this Puerto Rican slasher was filmed in Boston and Madrid by an Italian-based American producer and a Spanish director. Perhaps not surprisingly, it is a jumbled but heady brew of slasher movie violence, gore, bad acting, memorable dialogue and disco music.

Similarly, Jim Sotos's *Sweet 16* is memorable for its cheesiness. A new girl in town, the 15-year-old Melissa (Aleisa Shirley) is a big hit with the local boys. The trouble is any boy who takes a liking to

her ends up dead. The teenage kids of the local sheriff – including a heroically bad Nancy Drew–like character played by Dana Kimmell, who made this before *Friday the 13th Part 3* – decide to take matters into their own hands to stop the killings before Melissa's 16th birthday. Practically every slasher cliché is hammered into submission. The only way it really stands out from the rest of the pack is the fact that the victims at the end of the killer's knife are all male. Made in 1981, it sat on the shelf until late 1983 before getting released.

As the slasher market began to slump, filmmakers became more inventive with their plots. Robert Hiltzik's *Sleepaway Camp* caused something of a splash on its release. Angela (Felissa Rose) is a strange young girl sent to summer camp by her eccentric aunt; however, soon after her arrival, violent and bizarre accidents begin to claim the lives of her fellow campers. It is an unsubtle if occasionally surprising blend of *Friday the 13th* and teen sex comedies such as *Porky's*.

The fact that many of the protagonists – and victims – were barely pubescent also set it apart from earlier camp slashers. Despite the tender ages of much of the cast, the film is a heady brew of bad acting, implied paedophilia and violent murder. Of course, the reason the film is so well remembered is a twist ending that transcends the juvenile nature of the previous 90 minutes. Angela is actually a boy who has been forced to live his life as a girl, resulting in violent psychosis. The

Far left Dutch video artwork for *Sweet Sixteen*.

final shot of a naked Angela holding the severed head of another teen and staring dementedly out of the screen with an open-mouthed grin is certainly creepy and unexpectedly powerful.

By 1983, pretty much every scenario and calendar date had been snapped up and used (and recycled) by slasher moviemakers. So it must have seemed like a great idea to take that 'hoary old ghost house built atop an Indian burial ground' movie cliché and turn it into a 'stalk 'n' slash' (although this had already been done in 1980 in *Ghost Dance*). From prolific low-budget filmmaker Fred Olen Ray, *Scalps* is not without its cheesy charms. An unlikely-looking group of archaeological students become possessed and are killed while on a dig. Ray boasted that *Scalps* – and especially the gory scalping special effects – was one of the most censored films in history. It got a limited theatrical release in 1984.

Another slasher film attempting to sell itself on the gore ticket was Buddy Cooper's cheap and remarkably nasty *The Mutilator*. A young boy accidentally kills his mother with his father's gun. Fast-forward several years and the boy – now a college student – is asked by his nearly estranged father to close up his summer house on the beach. He sets off with a group of friends, who are killed off, as the classic tag line says, 'By sword, by pick, by axe, bye bye!' It was eventually released to some theatres unrated, after being slapped with an X rating by the MPAA (thanks to Mark Shostrom's graphic gore effects).

However, the film encountered problems finding bookings in theatres that had a blanket ban on unrated material, which was associated with hard-core pornography. Cooper went back and got an R rating for the film with cuts, but this – quite literally – ripped the guts from the movie. Finding himself without an audience, the director of *The Mutilator* lost a lot of money.

Mountaintop Motel Massacre was blessed with a great title and tagline – but sadly these were the only memorable things about this oddball production that sat on the shelf until 1986.

The first slasher film made directly for the home-video market was made in 1983. The plot of *Sledgehammer* is simplicity itself. A ragtag bunch of teens decide to hold a party at a remote house where sledgehammer murders happened 10 years ago. To no one's great surprise – certainly not the viewer's – the murders start afresh. In a nice bit of role reversal, the last man standing takes off his shirt to take on the killer for no other reason than to show off his six-pack (which could have something to do with the fact that he was *Playgirl* Man of the Month centrefold in March 1984). Shot for just $40,000, *Sledgehammer* made the most of the comparatively cheap technology – and a subgenre that was always cost conscious found an even thriftier avenue to go down.

1984 – THE END OF THE GOLDEN AGE

By 1984 the subgenre appeared to be on its last legs. Production of slashers had plummeted, and a whiff of desperation surrounded many of those that did go ahead.

Below and far right American poster artwork for *Friday the 13th: The Final Chapter,* and American poster artwork for *Splatter University* (*right*).

The major studios all but abandoned a subgenre that only a few years earlier had been a very profitable cash cow. Although it was rare to see slasher movies on the big screen, reissues and new video productions increasingly brought the subgenre to a whole new generation. Of course, as any aficionado of the slasher knows, the bogeyman never dies – and the subgenre wasn't ready to vanish completely off the radar just yet.

THE HIGHS OF 1984 . . .

Perhaps judging the public mood – and despite the impressive box office of *Part 3* in 1982 – the makers of *Friday the 13th: The Final Chapter* seemed ready to bring the saga of Camp Crystal Lake to a close.

There was a palpable

'If Nancy doesn't wake up screaming she won't wake up at all . . .'

– A Nightmare on Elm Street

sense of anticipation on how it would all end. Of course, knowing not to mess with a successful formula, the filmmakers closely adhered to the previous three films' template. Another group of highly sexed teenagers come to party at the remote lakeside setting, and nearby is another teenager (eventual Final Girl Kimberly Beck) and her younger special-effects-obsessed brother (future teen pinup Corey Feldman). Jason rises from the dead and, perhaps unsurprisingly, leaves a trail of bodies on the way back from the morgue to his old stomping ground to carry on where he left off. Joseph Zito – who previously directed *The Prowler* – did not have a lot of room to manoeuvre now that the formula was set in stone. However, to his credit, *The Final Chapter* has a nice gothic feel all of its own and satisfies with the now pleasingly familiar mixture of light relief, T&A and shock. Tom Savini returned to ostensibly kill off the monster. Scaring up a massive $32 million at the domestic box office, it was clear that this wasn't to be the end of the series after all – even if audiences at the time were understandably naive enough to believe that it would be.

. . . AND THE LOWS

At the other end of the spectrum was Troma's *Splatter University* – quite possibly the nadir of the subgenre and almost the final nail in its coffin. It is strictly amateur night at the morgue. Not able to decide whether it is a horror film or a comedy – it turns into the worst kind of misanthropic mess. Still, with characteristic optimism, Troma ordered 200 prints for the film's theatrical release.

Coming in at a close second to the bottom of the barrel is the zero-budget *Movie House Massacre*, which has usherettes stalked and slashed after a cinema is reopened. The killer is a hardly scary octogenarian in a tuxedo, who simply dodders up to his victims and stabs them bloodlessly. Hopeless as a horror movie, it works best when veering – purely intentionally – into John Waters's territory. Made by Rick Sloane – hiding under the pseudonym Alice Rayley – he somehow managed to persuade the super-talented

"THE MOST TERRIFYING FILM OF THE YE
– Rick Sullivan, Gor

Earn a Higher Degree in Terror!

LLOYD KAUFMAN / MICHAEL HERZ
Present

SPLATTER UNIVERSITY

Where The School Colors Are Blood Red...

Starring FRANCINE FORBES · CATHY LACOMMARE · DICK BIEL · DENISE TEXE
and JIM GRIB · Music by CHRIS BURKE · Songs by 'Th
Directors of Photography FRED COHEN and JOHN MICHAELS · Associate Producer MILJAN PETER ILICH · Di
Produced by RICHARD W. HAINES · AQUIFILM CO. PICTURE Released by TROMA, INC.
©RICHARD W. HAINES PRODUCTIONS, INC.

R RESTR

Below and far right
Students training
for the Olympics
are murdered by a
javelin-throwing killer
in *Fatal Games*;
American poster
artwork for *Silent
Madness* (right).

Mary Woronov to star in this stinker.
Despite its setting, it is unlikely that *Movie House Massacre* ever saw the big screen.

. . . AND THOSE THAT DESERVED TO FARE BETTER

The Canadian production *Evil Judgment* is a slasher-cum-conspiracy thriller that actually originated from the hallowed slasher year of 1981 but sat on the shelf until 1984, before vanishing into undeserved obscurity. This gritty, off-kilter tale has a down-on-her-luck waitress caught up in a series of gory murders. The black-gloved killer nods towards the *giallo* – as does the Italian-sounding name of the director, Claudio Castravelli.

The 1980s rock–slasher hybrid was never going to be free of cheese, but *Rocktober Blood*, from Beverly Sebastian, the director of proto-slasher *The Single Girls*, has more than the stench of dairy about it. A rock singer flips outs one night and kills everyone, except his girlfriend (Donna Scoggins), at a recording studio. Her testimony sends him to the electric chair, but after she takes over singing duties with the band, it appears that the shock rocker is back from the dead.

For the most part *Rocktober Blood* is a trashy delight. With touches such as the killer holding his breath underwater in a Jacuzzi to snag a victim, it's clearly not aiming to be a believable thriller. It got a brief theatrical run before finding its rightful home on video.

Nearly as cheesy is *Fatal Games*. Produced under the title *The Killing Touch* in 1983, it has an unusual pedigree, having been cowritten and coproduced by Rafael Buñuel (the son of the originator of cinematic surrealism Luis Buñuel). Also, Christopher Mankiewicz (the son of the director of high-profile Hollywood fare such as 1950's *All About Eve*) starred in, cowrote and coproduced the film.

Perhaps hoping to recreate an iota of the success of Jason's 3D outing in *Friday the 13th Part 3*, the makers of *Silent Madness* also opted for the third dimension for their slasher so they could wiggle and throw all kinds of sharp instruments at the audience. It was directed by Simon Nuchtern – presumably with more than a little tongue in his cheek. Instead of a homicidal maniac escaping from an asylum, one is released

Olympic Hopefuls are competing in the...

FATAL GAMES

IMPACT FILMS PRESENTS A MICHAEL ELLIOT FILM
SALLY KIRKLAND · LYNN BANASHEK · SEAN MASTERSON · TEAL ROBERTS · MICHAEL O'LEARY
LYNN ANN WILLIAMS · ANGELA BENNETT · MELISSA PROPHET
AUDETTA MURPHY · MICHAEL ELLIOT · CHRISTOPHER MANKIEWICZ

due to a computer error. He returns to the sorority house, where he apparently carried out a massacre with a nail gun some years before after being spanked and humiliated by the sorority sisters. *Silent Madness* was also released flat to some screens, which made the phoniness of the 3D effects even more apparent.

The lead actor of TV's successful series *The Partridge Family*, Danny Bonaduce starred in the obscure *Deadly Intruder* and rather appropriately has his head shoved through a TV.

It is hard to say what so offended movie-going patrons in 1984, who reputedly picketed *Silent Night, Deadly Night*'s opening with placards reading, 'Deck the halls with holly – not bodies!' It wasn't the first time Santa had been portrayed as psychotic. Perhaps TV commercials showing him swinging an axe with the tagline, *'He knows when you've been naughty!'* upset parents of young children. However, *Silent Night, Deadly Night* is too cheesy to be really offensive. Released to American movie theatres in time for Christmas, the original distributor, TriStar, found that not all publicity is good publicity, with persistent

HE'S OUT NOW...

The Terro has just begun!

SILENT MADNESS

IN 3-D

An AIMI PICTURES, INC. Release
A MAG ENTERPRISES and GREGORY EARLS Production
of a film by SIMON NUCHTERN
SILENT MADNESS
Starring Belinda Montgomery • Viveca Lindfors • Sydney Lassick
Screenplay By Robert Zimmerman and William P. Milling   Director of Photography Gerald Feil

Below and right Nancy is menaced by the man of her dreams, Freddy Krueger, in *A Nightmare on Elm Street.*

Far right British promotional artwork for *A Nightmare on Elm Street.*

carol-singing mothers forcing one Bronx cinema to pull it a week into its run. Widespread outrage by theatre owners and the press led to the film being pulled from other cinemas across the country – but lack of box-office figures, despite all of the publicity, probably also had something to do with it (it earned less than $2.5 million in its initial run).

A NIGHTMARE ON ELM STREET

While interest in the subgenre had waned considerably, Wes Craven's *A Nightmare on Elm Street* seemed to come out of left field and threatened to revitalize the slasher movie. Craven had toyed with the subgenre before with *Deadly Blessing* (1981); however, he was frustrated that the subgenre he had arguably helped create had so far not benefited him financially. Having developed what would become *A Nightmare on Elm Street* since 1981, Craven knew that time was fast running out, as the subgenre looked to be all but dead in the water within a year. He had little idea that his soon-to-be iconic bogeyman, the hideously scarred Freddy Krueger, would catch the imaginations of audiences worldwide (see review on page 197).

A Nightmare on Elm Street, and especially Krueger, became a cultural phenomenon. On a budget of just $1.8 million, which

Below A young Johnny Depp is no match for Freddy in *A Nightmare on Elm Street*.

Far right A curiously phallic American poster for *The Initiation*.

it earned back during its first week, the film grossed $25.5 million at the domestic box office and launched one of horror's most successful franchises. It also helped establish its studio, New Line Cinema, as a force to be reckoned with in Hollywood – not to mention also saving it from bankruptcy. The studio is still referred to as 'The House That Freddy Built'.

A Nightmare on Elm Street started a craze of surreal slasher movies that mixed reality and dreams. Perhaps hoping to ride the early wave, New World Pictures finally released the 1983 slasher *The Initiation* to theatres in December 1984. Daphne

Zuniga is plagued by what she thinks are nightmares (in fact they are repressed memories). It culminates in a shopping mall during pledge night, where the young coeds and their boyfriends fight for their lives against a mysterious killer – Zuniga's insane twin sister. As the last slasher movie released theatrically during the Golden Age, it provides a nice symmetry: the debt to *Halloween* is obvious, but *The Initiation* also stars Vera Miles, who played Marion Crane's sister in *Psycho*. However, Hitchcock's film didn't feature a scene with someone dressed as a giant penis attending a fraternity party.

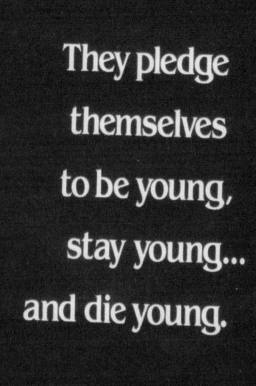

They pledge
themselves
to be young,
stay young...
and die young.

THE
INITIATION

...the night new blood is pledged.

"THE INITIATION"
Starring VERA MILES   CLU GULAGER
JAMES READ   Introducing DAPHNE ZUNIGA
Written by CHARLES PRATT, JR.
Executive Producers BRUCE LANSBURY and JOCK GAYNOR
Produced by SCOTT WINANT   Directed by LARRY STEWART
NEW WORLD PICTURES

INTERNATIONAL SLASHING (1978-84)

While the slasher movie had many international influences prior to *Halloween*, the boom in 'stalk 'n' slash' that followed was mostly made up of American and a few Canadian examples. However, other countries around the globe were also getting in on the act.

BRITAIN

Surprisingly, given how much Britain helped shape the subgenre, slasher movies from the United Kingdom during this period were few and far between.

Released in the same year as *Halloween, Killer's Moon* pitted stranded schoolgirls against four escaped mental patients on acid. *The Playbird Murders* (1978) was studio Tigon's update of proto-slasher *Cover Girl Killer*. Models are killed (and their body-count number put on their heads in lipstick). There were also the little-seen slasher shorts: hoodlums run amuck in a theatre in *The Last Night* (1983) and in the rurally based *Sleepwalker* (1984).

Don't Open Till Christmas (1984) rounded off the British contribution to the Golden Age, but it wasn't a particularly distinguished swansong. In a twist on the killer Santa, someone is slaying London's Santas. One has his face burnt off while roasting chestnuts, and another has his penis lopped off in a urinal.

AUSTRALIA

In the early 1970s sex comedies proliferated in the country as Ozploitation – low-budget exploitation movies. By the late 1970s Australian filmmakers turned their attention to the profitable slasher in the wake of the financial success of *Halloween*. The first, *Snapshot* (1979), wore its heart on its sleeve – despite not really being a slasher movie as such – by being brazenly released in the States as *Day After Halloween*. Expecting a continuation of the Michael Myers saga audiences must have been surprised when confronted by a psycho driving a Mr. Whippy ice cream van.

Easily the best Australian slasher movie made during this time was Tony Williams's *Next of Kin* (1982). A young woman is drawn into a web of murder and intrigue when she returns to the nursing home run by her late mother. It works especially well, juxtaposing the gruffness of rural Australia with Grand Guignol gothic.

However, if this was the best that Austrialia had to offer, then psychotic-handyman-versus-pop-star opus *Lady Stay Dead* (1981) must surely be the worst.

P. J. Soles – Lynda in *Halloween* – made her return to the subgenre in the ludicrous *Innocent Prey* (1984), from writer-director Colin Eggleston, who also wrote the Australian theatre-based slasher *Nightmares* (1980). Needless to say, it wasn't as accomplished as Carpenter's film. Soles does well, though, moving into pole position as the Final Girl. She is, however, hampered by one of the worst perms ever committed to celluloid.

ITALY

In Italy the popularity of the *giallo* had long since diminished. However, there were a number of notable exceptions, including Dario Argento's *Tenebre* (1982). Also Lamberto Bava's *A Blade in the Dark* (*La casa con la scala nel buio*, 1983), in which a composer tries to score a horror movie, as people begin to die for real.

Both are perfect examples of films that satisfy as *gialli* but also show the influence of the then in-vogue American slasher.

Influenced even further by the American slasher movie was Italian director Joe D'Amato. His *Antropophagus* (1980) has a group of hapless tourists pursued by a cannibalistic madman on a Greek island. Following it was the director's remake-cum-sequel *Absurd* (*Rosso sangue*, 1981). George Eastman again plays a variation on the same monster who escapes from a hospital and kills everyone he comes across. *Absurd* is very much removed from the *giallo*, taking its inspiration directly from *Halloween* and American gore movies.

EVERYONE HAS A SLASHER

For a while it seemed as if every country wanted some slasher action. Hong Kong had the entertaining Argento-inspired *He Lives by Night* (*Ye jing hun*, 1982), which finds a transvestite stalking a female radio host. New Zealand (in an Australian coproduction) made its own dead-teenager movie, *Dead Kids* (1981), set in the United States and featuring teenagers turned into murderers by demented scientists.

From director Hans Hatwig, *Blödaren* (1983) was billed as the first Swedish slasher flick. Sadly, it isn't great. Spanish director Jesus Franco gave us the West German *Bloody Moon* (*Die Säge des Todes*, 1981), which saw girls at a language school getting sliced and diced.

Brazil produced *Shock: Evil Entertainment* (*Shock: Diversão diabólica*, 1982), in which a psycho in shiny black boots stalks a group of rock musicians and their girlfriends at a lakeside recording studio.

Even South Africa got in on the act with the truly bizarre *The Demon* (1979), featuring Cameron Mitchell as a demented private investigator with extrasensory perception on the trail of the eponymous claw-handed villain – a full five years before anyone had even heard of the now-famous Freddy Krueger and his iconic appendage.

VIDEO HELL AND THE FRANCHISES (1985–95)

By 1985, the slasher movie was almost in the doldrums, but it didn't curl up and die – the video revolution was around the corner. Except for a few successful franchises and mainstream thrillers, the subgenre seemed condemned to straight-to-video hell.

Right American video artwork for *Blood Cult.*

Without the backing of major studios or their willingness to pick up independent features for theatrical release, the slasher movie entered its wilderness years. The video revolution had given new life to all movies, but along with pornography, horror was arguably the most popular genre for home viewing. And slasher movies came back to scare with new vigour, courtesy of hulking VCRs. Although the financial returns were down, the potential to turn a profit – especially with the cheaper new medium of video – was too difficult to resist for many. Mirroring punk rock, the slasher movie took the DIY idea that 'anyone could do it' to new heights. Anyone *could* do it, but unfortunately, few could do it well.

To list all of the slasher movies made post-1985 would take another book and a half. However, starting at the very bottom of the barrel is *Blood Cult* (1985), which features some anonymous wacko carving up coeds with a highly polished meat cleaver on a small Midwestern campus. So

bad that it had to rely on the advertising gimmick that it was the first shot-on-video slasher movie (even though it wasn't), it has perhaps the most unattractive cast in slasher movie history. Also showing the paucity of budget and imagination was the gory and sleazy *The Ripper* (also 1985), which has a short cameo from special-effects guru Tom Savini as the title character. Other lo-fi extravaganzas stinking up the shelves in video stores included *Spine* (1986), *Truth or Dare? A Critical Madness* (1986), and many, many others . . .

'Anyone could do it, but . . . few could do it well.'

Above Another victim in *Friday the 13th: A New Beginning*.

The mid-1980s also saw a fresh wave of sequel mania with many filmmakers preferring to exploit an already-known title rather than go into uncharted territory with new ideas. Even Wes Craven wasn't above this when he made the enjoyably dreadful *The Hills Have Eyes Part 2* (1985). Most definitely a step down from *A Nightmare on Elm Street*, it features the same mutant family that terrorized the cast in his 1977 original attacking dirt bikers. Craven has reputedly disowned the film, and it is perhaps most notable for having a scene where even a dog has a flashback.

Proving you just can't keep a good psycho down – especially when the box office is booming – a new chapter of *Friday the 13th* appeared in 1985. The cheekily titled *Friday the 13th: A New Beginning* was an attempt to breath new life into the presumed moribund franchise. Jason is actually dead, and it is a copycat killer offing kids at a retreat for troubled teenagers. The film remained hugely profitable for Paramount, but audiences felt duped and wanted Jason back for real. The box office fell accordingly to $21,930,418.

After the huge success of the first part, it came as no surprise to anyone when *A Nightmare on Elm Street Part 2: Freddy's Revenge* (1985) was announced. What did surprise many was its relatively left-field approach – and it was missing Wes Craven. Jack Sholder – who had previously helmed *Alone in the Dark* – had reputedly not wanted to make 'just another slasher movie', and this film distinguishes itself from the pack by having a male protagonist (Mark Patton) and homoerotic undertones. However, it was widely criticized for losing much of the dream logic that had made the first film so interesting. Despite this, it made an impressive $29,999,213 on a $3 million budget – and, more importantly, it marked the point when the *Nightmare* franchise took the crown from the *Friday* franchise as the most profitable. It also marked the point that fantasy slashers – inspired by the *A Nightmare on Elm Street* series – began to become more prevalent. *Dreamaniac* (1986), *Bad Dreams*, *Deadly Dreams* and *Dream Demon* (all three 1988) are just a handful of genre movies that attempted to share the limelight with the emerging franchise.

By 1986, the subgenre was having its bloody cake and trying to eat it too, satirizing itself while also attempting to work as straightforward slasher movies.

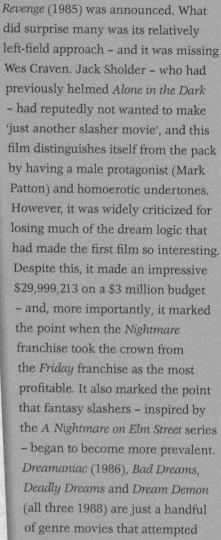

Guess who's going to be the life of the party?

APRIL FOOL'S DAY

...A cut above the rest.

ES PRESENTS A HOMETOWN FILMS PRODUCTION · APRIL FOOLS DAY · MUSIC BY CHARLES BERNSTEIN
BACH · PRODUCED BY FRANK MANCUSO JR. DIRECTED BY FRED WALTON · A PARAMOUNT PICTURE
SOUNDTRACK ALBUM AVAILABLE ON VARÈSE SARABANDE RECORDS AND CASSETTES. DOLBY STEREO PANAVISION

Far left Freddy Krueger: an unlikely screen idol.

Left and below American poster artwork for *April Fool's Day* and *Friday the 13th Part VI: Jason Lives.*

Also decidedly low-rent in nature was *Evil Laugh*, filmed in 1986 but released in 1988. It is notable for being what *Scream* would be 10 years later: an irony-fuelled yet affectionate take on the subgenre. Among the doomed youngsters within a house is a character who makes self-referential remarks, neatly mirroring the character Randy in Wes Craven's film.

Rounding off the newly self-aware breed of slashers was *Friday the 13th Part VI: Jason Lives* (1986). Jason – albeit a zombie version – is back and stalking campers anew. The character of Tommy Jarvis returns to battle Jason at his old stomping ground. Thankfully, it works as both a straightforward slasher film and a postmodern spin on the subgenre, with a witty James Bond parody in the opening credits and one character saying to another, 'I've seen enough horror movies to know that any freak standing in the middle of the road with a mask on isn't friendly!' However, it wasn't enough to prevent the franchise's still sizable profits shrinking further with a domestic take of $19,472,057.

The next year, Freddy continued his ascent with *A Nightmare on*

Director Fred Walton returned to the subgenre with *April Fool's Day* (1986), which, as the name suggests, revolves around an elaborate hoax – the murders that plague a group of friends on an island are, in fact, faked. A riff on Agatha Christie's *And Then There Were None* and many of the clichés of the slasher, it was released by Paramount, keen to wring more money from the subgenre. It worked; the movie earned over $12 million at the domestic box office.

JASON LIVES

FRIDAY THE 13th PART

KILL OR BE KILLED.

PARAMOUNT PICTURES PRESENTS A TERROR, INC. PRODUCTION FRIDAY THE 13TH, PART VI:
MUSIC BY HARRY MANFREDINI · DIRECTOR OF PHOTOGRAPHY JON R. KRANHOU
WRITTEN BY TOM MCLOUGHLIN · PRODUCED BY DON BEHRNS · DIRECTED BY TOM MCL
A PARAMOUNT PICTURE R

Below American poster artwork for *A Nightmare on Elm Street 3: Dream Warriors.*

Elm Street 3: Dream Warriors (1987). Reuniting Heather Langenkamp and John Saxon from the first film, it was widely considered an improvement on the first sequel, and audiences agreed with a huge $44,793,222 haul at the box office.

Acknowledging Freddy's allure in the *Nightmare on Elm Street* franchise,

Friday the 13th Part VII: The New Blood (1988) went supernatural, taking psychokinetic *Carrie* as its main inspiration. A teenage girl accidentally resurrects Jason from a watery grave and then spends the rest of the movie using her mind to fling sharp objects at him. It made just less than the last instalment, with a take of $19,170,001. However, even as Freddy continued to assail the box office, he increasingly lost his power to scare, becoming more of a wise-cracking horror buffoon than a genuine bogeyman. Despite this, *A Nightmare on Elm Street 4: The Dream Master* (1988) drew in an impressive $49,369,899.

The year 1988 also saw the return of the Shape in *Halloween 4: The Return of Michael Myers*, with Myers emerging from a coma and returning to Haddonfield to hunt down his young niece, Jamie (Danielle Harris). Respectfully directed by Dwight H. Little, it takes care to recreate the atmosphere of the original, if not quite managing to replicate the scares. Missing the input of Jamie Lee Curtis (who cameos via a Polaroid), it is at least bolstered by the return of Donald Pleasence as the increasingly demented Loomis. Released just before Halloween and proving that interest in the big-league psychos was still there, *Halloween 4* sat astride the top of the American box office for two weeks. Its total domestic gross of $17,768,757 meant that this ghoulish holiday was far from over.

Surprisingly, the old masters of mayhem were challenged by a pint-sized competitor

YOU THINK YOU'LL GET OUT ALIVE, YOU MUST BE DREAMING.

A Nightmare 3 ON ELM STREET DREAM WARRIORS

A ROBERT SHAYE Production A NIGHTMARE ON ELM STREET: PART 3: DREAM WARRIORS JOHN SAXON · DICK CAVETT and ZSA ZSA GABOR Starring HEATHER LANGENKAMP · PATRICIA ARQUETTE · LARRY FISHBURNE · PRISCILLA POINTER Featuring *Dokken* on ELEKTRA RECORDS and ROBERT ENGLUND as FREDDY KRUEGER WES CRAVEN and STEPHEN DIENER Line Producer RACHEL TALALAY

in *Child's Play* (1988). Taking its lead from killer-doll opuses such as *Dead of Night* (1945) and *Trilogy of Terror* (1975), it exploits childhood fears when a 'Chucky' doll is possessed by the spirit of a murderer and terrorizes a young boy and his mother. Proving that audiences still respond to fresh ideas, it made $33,244,684 – enough to generate two sequels in 1990 and 1991.

THE END OF THE SUBGENRE?

Perhaps the series' nadir, *Friday the 13th Part VIII: Jason Takes Manhattan* (1989) took a fun idea – putting Jason Voorhees in New York City (the joke being that he fits in) – and had it defeated by budgetary limitations; most of the film takes place on the boat journey there. The box office produced a paltry $14,343,976. In a reversal of fortunes, Freddy also lost his sparkle in *A Nightmare on Elm Street: The Dream Child* (1989); it proved to be a sequel too far, taking $22,168,359, which was less than half of what its predecessor took the year before. The year saw another turning point for the subgenre with *Halloween 5: The Revenge of Michael Myers* (1989); it had been hurried into production after the success of the previous instalment. Despite some nice gothic touches, it was a rush job, and it shows. Audience interest dwindled; the movie made just $11,642,254 at the American box office.

Just as *Friday the 13th: The Final Chapter* had hoodwinked audiences, they fell for it again with *Freddy's Dead: The Final Nightmare* (1991). Ostensibly the last in the series, it was, of course, nothing of the kind. Sadly though, audiences found Freddy more a buffoon than the sinister figure he had been in the first film. The anticlimactic and frankly subpar 3D used in the last 10 minutes was oddly fitting for a franchise that had clearly run out of creative steam. Still, with a box-office take of $34,872,033, it was obvious that Freddy would be back to haunt dreams again.

Below Advance American poster artwork for *Friday the 13th Part VIII: Jason Takes Manhattan*.

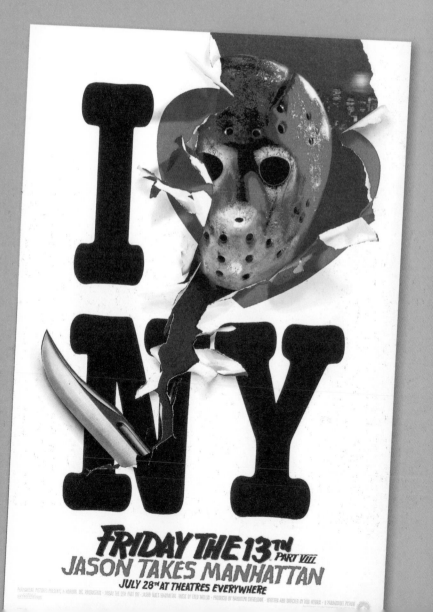

SLASHER MOVIES' INFLUENCE ON THE MAINSTREAM

While outside the franchise juggernauts that steamrollered through the 1980s, mainstream Hollywood didn't make slasher movies in the purest sense. But that didn't stop them from raiding the subgenre's toy box for ideas to pep up pedestrian thrillers. From creative body counts and shock jumps to killers who weren't really dead and subjective camera work, the slasher movie's influence was widely felt – but not given any credit, of course.

Jagged Edge (1985) led the move into the mainstream, as teenagers gave way to older victims (see American poster art at far right). The first five minutes are pure slasher, with POV shots leading to the murder of a woman by a knife-wielding maniac on a dark and stormy night. However, much of the rest, except for a short burst of slasher-style thrills at its close, is standard thriller fare. It was a sizable hit, with over $40 million at the domestic box office.

Adrian Lyne's *Fatal Attraction* (1987) was another example of how the slasher moved into the mainstream. While most of the film is a fairly orthodox thriller (albeit more erotically charged than most), it is the ending that marks out its magpie nature. Originally, the finale was more downbeat and subdued, but reshoots had the supposedly dead villain fly from a full bathtub like a screaming banshee. Anyone who has seen *Friday the 13th* will tell you that it is pure Camp Crystal Lake. The slasher shock ending propelled *Fatal Attraction* from a so-so thriller to a box-office champ as the second highest-grossing film in America in 1987, with an impressive domestic haul of $156,645,693.

Director Joseph Ruben (who directed *The Stepfather* in 1987) hit pay dirt with familial dysfunction in a polished variation on the subgenre. The idea of Julia Roberts in a slasher movie may seem absurd, but *Sleeping with the Enemy* (1991), which features Roberts as an abused wife trying everything to escape a violent husband, jettisons routine thriller and borrows all the tricks in the book during a frenzied finale.

Towards the mid-1990s mainstream thrillers continued borrowing elements from slashers. Among them was a psycho nanny in *The Hand That Rocks the Cradle* (1992), a psycho roommate in *Single White Female* (1992), and a psycho secretary in *The Temp* (1993). All had female villains, as oestrogen briefly beat out testosterone in the celluloid rage stakes. The subgenre continued to

diversify within the mainstream, and it blossomed in the low-budget field of straight-to-video terror. Soon, widespread public interest all but waned for the genre, which was mired in cliché and repetition.

CANDYMAN BREAKS THE MOULD

An anomaly compared to the endless cycle of increasingly cheesy slasher sequels was Bernard Rose's intelligent and visually striking *Candyman* (1992). Based on the short story by Clive Barker, it has the eponymous villain – played by Tony Todd, the first black slasher movie antihero – who appears and kills those foolish enough to say his name in the mirror five times. It anticipated the films that took similar folklore as its hook, most notably *Urban Legend* (1998).

Atypically based in a deprived and black inner-city neighbourhood, it was also the inspiration for other markedly less-successful genre films that moved their location to a more urban setting, including *Hood of Horror* (2006). Its $25,792,310 takings at the box office was enough to generate two sequels in 1995 and 1999 – as well as arguably providing the impetus for the slashers' rebirth several years later, with films such as *New Nightmare* (1994) and *Scream* (1996).

New Line Cinema acquired the rights to the *Friday the 13th* franchise – with an eye on the inevitable *Freddy vs. Jason* monster mash that eventually came 10 years later – and attempted to breath new life into it with *Jason Goes to Hell: The Final Friday* (1993). The results were decidedly mixed, with an ill-advised body-hopping storyline. A mediocre box office of just $15,935,068 showed that audiences weren't yet hungry for the resurrection of Jason Voorhees.

Unexpectedly, Wes Craven – who had briefly revived the subgenre in 1984 with *A Nightmare on Elm Street* – was up to new yet familiar tricks with *New Nightmare* (1994). With a clever concept that was strikingly original at the time, Craven utilized characters from the *Nightmare* universe, including Heather Langenkamp and Robert Englund. They played themselves and were terrorized by the Freddy Krueger character, who had now crossed from reel life to real life.

With one eye on the financial successes of the past, it also had an eye on the future and single-handedly led to the subgenre's postmodern second coming with the release of yet another Craven film in 1996. *New Nightmare* was a meagre success with a $18,090,181 take at the box office.

Halloween: The Curse of Michael Myers (1995) was the famously troubled sixth instalment in the *Halloween* franchise. Sections were hurriedly re-shot after disastrous test screenings. It is at least notable for the last film appearance of genre stalwart Donald Pleasence. It made just $15,116,634.

Left The adaptation of Clive Barker's *Candyman* stood out in a sea of sequels.

INTERNATIONAL SLASHING (1985-95)

As general interest in the subgenre shrunk in the United States, it was the same story internationally. Production of slashers slowed – although they were briefly buoyed by the phenomenal success of the *Nightmare on Elm Street* series.

Below Bad perms and blades in this Mexican lobby card for Italian slasher *Bodycount*.

Far right British video artwork for *Don't Panic* and *Blood Tracks*.

MEXICO

Bucking the trend, Mexico stepped up production, including *Cemetery of Terror* (*Cementerio del terror*, 1985), *Don't Panic* (1987) and *Grave Robbers* (*Ladrones de tumbas*, 1990), all directed by the seemingly indefatigable Rubén Galindo Jr.,

with a typically heady mix of cheese and graphic violence. Pedro Galindo III's *Hell's Trap* (*Trampa infernal*, 1990), which sees a group of teenage campers threatened by a crazed ex-soldier, was still closely modelled on earlier American slasher movies.

CAMPAMENTO DEL TERROR

FORGET FREDDIE AND JASON

18

Don't Panic

THE REAL NIGHTMARE IS JUST BEGINNING!

COLOURBOX

THE MOUNTAINS ECHOED WITH THE SCREAMS OF

BLOOD TRACKS

18

SWEDEN

Blood Tracks (1985) from Sweden was deliciously demented, with a poodle-permed rock band and its groupies attacked by mutants during a photoshoot in the mountains. The scene in which a balloon-haired model tries to escape from the marauding killer on a snowmobile is worth every penny of the price of the rental fee alone. Fashion models pitted against monsters is perhaps the ultimate in trash aesthetics – even if the film doesn't quite live up to it.

Right and far right American video artwork for *Goodnight, God Bless.*

ITALY AGAIN

The production of *gialli* also decreased significantly since its early 1970s heyday. However, they did periodically appear, with Dario Argento, Lamberto Bava and Ruggero Deodato still peddling their craft with increasingly mixed results.

Former Argento acolyte Michele Soavi perhaps scored the best slasher-*giallo* crossover with his feature début *StageFright: Aquarius* (*Deliria*, 1987). The plot is simplicity itself: an actor escapes from an asylum and then, wearing a giant owl mask, stalks actors at a theatre during rehearsals. The juxtaposition of the single-mindedness of the American slasher movie and the undeniable stylishness of the Italian *giallo* struck subgenre gold. However, Deodato's backwoods slasher, *Bodycount* (*Camping del terrore*, 1987), jettisons all Italian qualities and is almost slavish in its attempts to be American.

UNITED KINGDOM, SPAIN AND JAPAN

The United Kingdom scored its own goal with the dreadful killer-priest opus *Goodnight, God Bless* (1987). From Spain came the surreal *Anguish* (*Angustia*, 1987). Set in a cinema, it played upon the same audience fears as Lamberto Bava's tremendously entertaining monster mash *Demons* (*Dèmoni*, 1986): that something lurks at the multiplex. Surprisingly, despite the huge popularity of North American slasher movies in Japan, there were precious few examples coming out of the country, although the nastily surreal *Evil Dead Trap* (*Shiryô no wana*, 1988) is an interesting anomaly.

AUSTRALIA

Last – and certainly least – is the mind-bogglingly awful *Houseboat Horror* (1989) from Australia. An abomination from start to finish, the cast is stalked by a hideously scarred madman. Perhaps only of interest is that it stars Alan Dale, who gets his head split in half with a machete but afterwards went on to a Hollywood career in films such as *Indiana Jones and the Kingdom of the Crystal Skull* (2008). Thankfully, *Symphony of Evil* (1987) and *Bloodmoon* (1990) went some way to alleviate the Antipodean shame.

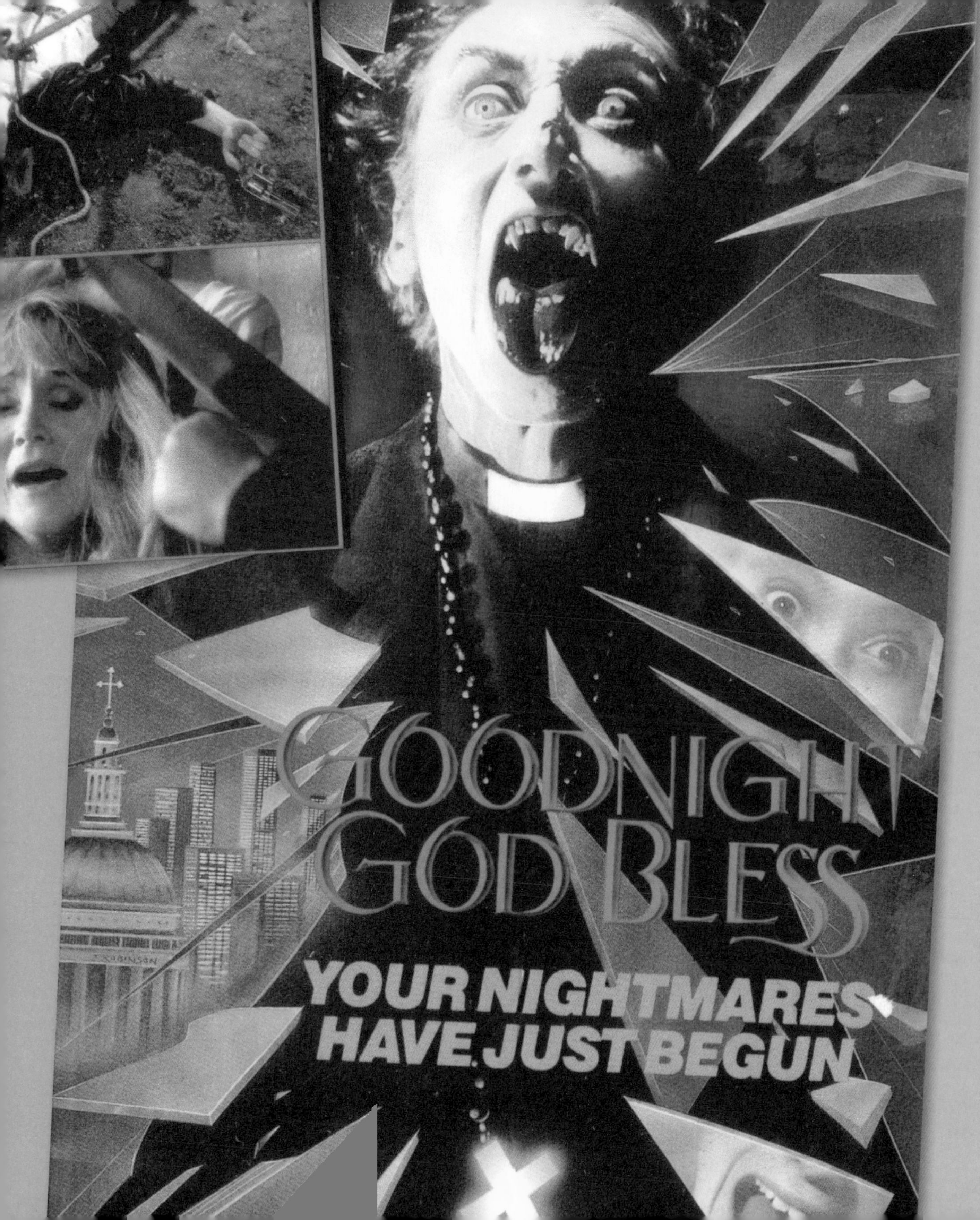
GOODNIGHT
GOD BLESS
YOUR NIGHTMARES
HAVE JUST BEGUN

SCREAM AND SCREAM AGAIN (1996 ONWARD)

By 1996, the slasher movie was pretty much dead in the water. Therefore, its surprising resurrection with *Scream* (1996) was proof that this really is the subgenre that just won't stay dead.

A box-office smash at the tail end of the year, *Scream* skillfully juggled postmodern humour and visceral horror – a case of being in the right place at the right time. It played on the nostalgia of those who had packed screens during the slasher's heyday in the early 1980s. It also appealed to a younger audience who saw their contemporaries sliced and diced by homicidal maniacs for the first time. In a decade where pop culture was cannibalizing itself, a film that exploited this and worked as a straightforward slasher was on target to be a runaway hit.

A NEW AGE IN SLASHERS

Scream was the brainchild of fledgling screenwriter Kevin Williamson, a self-confessed fan of Golden Age slashers. Originally entitled *Scary Movie*, the twist in *Scream* is that the teenage characters are well versed in slasher movie lore and know all the clichés, comparing scenes from their favourite subgenre movies to a series of brutal murders rocking their small town.

'Sidney, how does it feel to be almost brutally butchered?'

– Reporter, *Scream*

The fact that the audience was also aware of those same clichés added to the fun and helped propel the movie to a whopping domestic gross of $103,046,663 on a budget of just $14 million.

After touting the script around Hollywood, Williamson sold the rights to Miramax, which bought it for its new Dimension Films label. The makers of *Scream* secured something of a horror coup by tempting director Wes Craven aboard.

Despite being worn by different characters throughout the franchise, the killer in *Scream* is Ghostface, who sports a distorted mask based on the painting *The Scream* by Edvard Munch. Williamson

DON'T ANSWER THE PHONE. DON'T OPEN THE DOOR. DON'T TRY TO ESCAPE.

THE HIGHLY ACCLAIMED NEW THRILLER FROM WES CRAVEN

SCREAM

18

DAVID ARQUETTE   NEVE CAMPBELL   COURTENEY COX   MATTHEW LILLARD   ROSE McGOWAN   SKEET ULRICH   & DREW BARRYMORE

Above British poster artwork for *Scream*.

and Craven knew well not to make fun of their villain – a mistake that has sunk many a horror comedy. Ghostface, while not adverse to numerous pratfalls, remains suitably scary, while the humour comes from the characters' self-reflexive but well-placed paranoia.

As the subgenre had been exhausted financially by 1996, Miramax's original advertising distanced itself from it.

Hedging their bets, posters for the film announced *Scream* as a 'new thriller' from Craven. They didn't need to worry. The positive critical and financial reception to the film hinted that the subgenre was on its way back from the grave.

The stellar box-office turnout of Williamson's follow-up the next year, *I Know What You Did Last Summer* (1997), silenced those who presumed that *Scream*

If you're going
to bury the truth,
make sure
it stays buried.

I KNOW
WHAT YOU DID
LAST SUMMER

"More laughs and chills than SCREAM"

MANDALAY ENTERTAINMENT PRESENTS A NEAL H. MORITZ PRODUCTION "I KNOW WHAT YOU DID LAST SUMMER" MUSIC BY ALEX STEYERMARK
JENNIFER LOVE HEWITT SARAH MICHELLE GELLAR RYAN PHILLIPPE FREDDIE PRINZE, JR. JOHNNY GALECKI BRIGITTE WILSON
MUSIC BY JOHN DEBNEY EDITED BY STEVE MIRKOVICH, A.C.E. PRODUCTION DESIGNER GARRY WISSNER DIRECTOR OF PHOTOGRAPHY DENIS CROSSAN, B.S.C. BASED ON THE NOVEL BY WILLIAM S. BEASLEY BASED ON THE NOVEL BY LOIS DUNCAN SCREENPLAY BY KEVIN WILLIAMSON
mandalay ENTERTAINMENT R READ THE ARCHWAY PAPERBACK EXECUTIVE PRODUCERS NEAL H. MORITZ, ERIK FEIG AND STOKELY CHAFFIN DIRECTED BY JIM GILLESPIE

COLUMBIA
PICTURES

Right American
poster artwork for
*I Know What You
Did Last Summer.*

was a flash in the pan. Based loosely on
the Lois Duncan book of the same name,
four teenagers find themselves at the sharp
end of a psychotic fisherman's hook after
they try to cover up a potentially fatal
hit-and-run. Again, it acknowledged the

setup of films such as the original *Prom
Night,* where an accident is the catalyst
for later mayhem. Despite *Scream*'s
success, the film played it straight with
little pop-culture trickery. After a brief
critical holiday in the sun with *Scream,*
the slasher once again proved itself to be
critic proof as *I Know What You Did Last
Summer* deflected negative notices. If any
doubts remained that the slasher movie
had become hot property again, they were
shattered by the huge $72,586,134 haul at
the domestic box office.

Inevitably, *Scream 2* followed at the end
of 1997, and just as inevitably, it scored
big with a domestic haul of $101,363,301.
Reuniting much of the surviving cast
from the first film – not to mention Wes
Craven back in the director's chair – it
successfully combined straight scares with
postmodern quips about slasher movies
and the nature of sequels. Again written
by Kevin Williamson, this time *Scream 2*
took the dorm slashers of the early 1980s –
such as *Final Exam* – as inspiration. It also
owes a debt of gratitude to sorority slashers
such as *The House on Sorority Row*. Final
Girl Sidney Prescott tries to rebuild her life
at college only to find herself once again
at the centre of carnage, as students fall
victim to Ghostface once more.

Michael Myers returned in *Halloween
H20: 20 Years Later* (1998), spurred by the
subgenre's resurgence. Steve Miner, who
had helmed two of the *Friday the 13th*
sequels, was given the job of scaring the
Scream generation anew with the original

bogeyman. *Scream* writer Kevin Williamson was also involved, providing a treatment. The film was a direct sequel to *Halloween II,* ignoring all the sequels that followed, to the annoyance of many fans. This allowed famous Final Girl Jamie Lee Curtis to once again take on the role of Laurie Strode – here as an alcoholic headmistress of an exclusive school who is still haunted by the memories of her murderous brother. Despite John Carpenter not returning, the film did good business, if not quite *Scream* sized at the box office, bringing in a very respectable $55,041,738.

The goofier side of Golden Age slashers was celebrated by director Jamie Blanks's *Urban Legend* in 1998. Again college campus set, it used the clever premise that a killer was offing victims using methods described in urban legends. The parka-clad assassin is memorably sinister. However, the film was widely criticized as being too silly – which was rather missing the point, as anyone who has enjoyed the absurdities of films such as Golden Age slasher *Happy Birthday to Me* will tell you. It earned $38,072,438, which showed that perhaps the slasher movie was again losing its momentum at the box office.

The same year, the once-prolific Canada – which had produced Golden Age slasher classics such as the original *My Bloody Valentine* – made a comeback of sorts with *The Clown at Midnight.* The usual array of attractive teenagers are stalked and killed by a clown at a dilapidated opera house. Making a welcome return to the slasher was Margot Kidder, who ended her days at the sharp end of a glass ornament in the classic 1970s proto-slasher *Black Christmas.*

THE RETURN OF THE SEQUEL

After the success of *Halloween* and *Friday the 13th* in the late 1970s and early 1980s, the slasher movie was settling into a familiar pattern, with sequels getting made

Below What goes around comes around, and *Scream* was quickly followed by *Scream 2.*

for the most successful films and new franchises being born. *I Still Know What You Did Last Summer* (1999) saw Jennifer Love Hewitt return as a still-traumatized Julie James, who escaped the clutches of the hook-handed killer in the first film. She and her new friends are hoodwinked into accepting a vacation at a remote island hotel just closing for the season. In a move that surprised no one, they start dying one by one. *I Still Know What You Did Last Summer* was hated by critics and fans alike but actually captures the excitement and sheer, utter cheesiness that made some of the most popcornesque early 1980s slashers so much fun. I unashamedly adore it, especially the karaoke scene. Whoever had the idea to have Julie singing Gloria Gaynor's 'I Will Survive' only to see the words 'I Still Know' blink across the karaoke screen deserves some kind of cheddar medal. Audiences were still hooked, and the film took home a $40,002,112 domestic haul.

AND STILL MORE COME . . .

Displaying distinctively magpie tendencies was *Lovers Lane* (1999). Based on the urban legend, it has another hook-handed killer targeting a group of teens. It was influenced by Golden Age slashers, and its debt to *I Know What You Did Last Summer* is also clear. It starred

'Based on an urban legend, it has another hook-handed killer targeting a group of teens.'

Anna Faris, who went on to make a name for herself spoofing exactly these kind of movies in the phenomenally successful *Scary Movie* franchise. More interesting was the surrealistic *Kolobos* (1999), which is akin to *Big Brother* being shot by Dario Argento. In the film, a group of wannabe reality stars die within a booby-trapped house. It may have inspired the later *Saw* franchise (2004–), as well as other films that took the same central premise, such as *Voyeur.com* (2000) and *My Little Eye* (2002).

Cherry Falls (2000) put an interesting twist on the formula. Reversing the old subgenre adage that sex equals death, which had become such a cliché in Golden Age slashers, the teens in typical small town Americana are targeted by a killer who only kills virgins – leading to a mad rush to pop cherries left, right and centre.

Scream 3 (2000) finished the proposed trilogy with a distinct case of diminishing returns, at least creatively. In a typically self-referential manner, murders are plaguing the set of *Stab 3*, the latest in a series of films based on the events in the *Scream* franchise. Despite, or perhaps because of, the return of the surviving characters and Wes Craven at the helm, the film suffered from a smugness that dissipated the air of danger in the first two films. It was the only part of the *Scream* cycle not fully written by Kevin Williamson due to a clash of schedules. It was also the first of the franchise not to break the $100 million barrier at the domestic box office but did bring in a healthy $89,143,175.

Profits continued to shrink with *Urban Legends: Final Cut* (2000), in which film students are offed by a killer in a fencing mask (a disguise borrowed from Golden Age slasher *Graduation Day*). Directed by composer John Ottman and starring Hart Bochner (who memorably lost his head in *Terror Train*), it made a meagre profit on a haul of $21,468,807. Released the next year, *Valentine* (2001)

Far left Pretty faces lined up to die in *Urban Legend*.

Below And more pretty faces in *I Still Know What You Did Last Summer*.

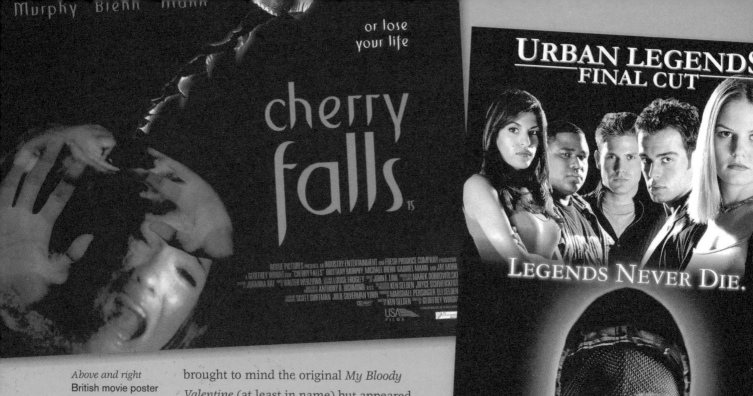

or lose
your life

cherry
falls 15

ROGUE PICTURES PRESENTS AN INDUSTRY ENTERTAINMENT AND FRESH PRODUCE COMPANY PRODUCTION
A GEOFFREY WRIGHT FILM "CHERRY FALLS" BRITTANY MURPHY, MICHAEL BIEHN, GABRIEL MANN AND JAY MOHR
CASTING JOHANNA RAY MUSIC WALTER WERZOWA COSTUME DESIGNER LOUISE FROGLEY EDITOR JOHN F. LINK PRODUCTION DESIGNER MAREK DOBROWOLSKI
CO-PRODUCER ANTHONY B. RICHMOND, B.S.C. EXECUTIVE PRODUCERS KEN SELDEN JOYCE SCHWEICKERT
PRODUCERS SCOTT SHIFFMAN JULIE SILVERMAN YORN WRITTEN BY KEN SELDEN DIRECTED BY GEOFFREY WRIGHT
USA FILMS

URBAN LEGENDS
FINAL CUT

LEGENDS NEVER DIE.

CUTTING-EDGE TERROR IS BACK.

Above and right
British movie poster
for *Cherry Falls*
and American DVD
artwork for *Urban
Legends: Final Cut.*

brought to mind the original *My Bloody Valentine* (at least in name) but appeared to show that the slasher boom had all but petered out on the big screen. Made by *Urban Legend* filmmaker Jamie Blanks, the movie has a group of now grown-up school friends stalked by a killer in a sinister cherub mask. It met with a wall of indifference from both critics and audiences, and its $20,384,136 domestic box-office take wasn't enough to cover its production budget.

REINVENTING THE GENRE

By 2002 the slasher movie seemed once again a spent force in mainstream cinema, leading to budgets dropping and subject matter diversifying. *Make a Wish* (2002) distinguished itself as the first lesbian slasher movie. In a subgenre where jiggling breasts are usually aimed at a male and largely adolescent audience,

horror and homosexuality may appear to be strange bedfellows. However, it is 'fear of the other' that underpins almost all horror tales, so it should really come as no surprise that there has been a 'queer' undercurrent in genre cinema from the beginning. Whereas it was once steeped in allegory, *Make a Wish* was one of a number of horror films that emerged primarily for a gay audience. It was followed by the entertaining *Hellbent* (2004), another gay slasher that features men at the West Hollywood Halloween Carnival being targeted by a psycho in a devil's mask armed with a sickle. There was even a gay porn version of *Scream* called *Moan* (1999), as well as *Camp Cuddly Pines Powertool Massacre* (2005), which was a porn riff on summer camp slaughter movies from the 1980s.

Golden Age slasher movies were infamous for killing off their black cast members early on (if they had black cast members at all), so to redress the balance, some made primarily for black audiences began to appear, such as *Killjoy* (2000), *Holla If I Kill You* (2003), *Holla* (2006) and *Somebody Help Me* (2007).

The year 2002 saw the return of Michael Myers in *Halloween: Resurrection*. Rick Rosenthal, the director of the first sequel, returned with a not-very-engaging reality TV–inspired story, with cameras placed around the infamous Myers house. Cue the return of the Shape and ensuing murders of intrepid teenagers. The ill-advised inclusion of a semicomic role by rapper Busta Rhymes almost brought down the film. It only distinguishes itself by killing off Jamie Lee Curtis' Laurie Strode, at least for now. Proving that there was still some goodwill towards the franchise, it scared up a respectable $30,354,442 domestically.

Not faring so well was *Jason X* (2002), which did little to bolster the slasher movie's flagging fortunes. The tenth *Friday the 13th* movie blasted Jason Voorhees into the future and into space, where, naturally, teenagers still succumb to their hormones. Despite some witty moments, including the holograms of horny campers enraging Jason, it failed to generate much excitement or interest. Its $13,121,555 at the domestic

Below left and below The subgenre faltered once again with *Valentine* but diversified with films such as *Hellbent*.

FROM THE CO-CREATOR OF "HALLOWEEN" AND THE EXECUTIVE PRODUCER OF "A NIGHTMARE ON ELM STREET"

HELLBENT

WHEN THE NIGHT BELONGS TO THE DEVIL, THE PARTY GOES TO HELL

Below and right
Slashers in space!
Jason X (*below*) and
psychos resurgent
in *Freddy vs. Jason*
(*right*).

Far right South
Korean DVD artwork
for *Wrong Turn*.

box office barely covered production costs
and made it the lowest-grossing film in the
series.

However, a year is a long time in
cinema, and the *Friday the 13th* franchise
was spectacularly resurgent with the
barnstorming *Freddy vs. Jason* (2003).
Mooted since 1986, the battle of the
psychos finally came to fruition under
the expectant eye of New Line Cinema.
Chinese director Ronny Yu added an
interesting spin visually. Robert Englund
donned the deadly glove once again,
but Ken Kirzinger replaced long-term
Jason Kane Hodder, much to many fans'
dismay. As to be expected, an unlucky
group of teens find
themselves in the
dangerous fighting
grounds – the
filmmakers wisely
took the action
back to Camp
Crystal Lake and
Elm Street – and
end their days in
the time-honoured
tradition. As
Scream before it,
the film played
off nostalgia and
interest from new
fans to the tune
of a $82,622,655
domestic take.

Making only a
shade less was

the remake *The Texas Chainsaw Massacre*
(2003), which generated $80,571,655
domestically. Set in the early 1970s (when
the original was made), it signalled a
significant change from the days when
franchises wore their increasing digits as
badges of honour. That year, 2003, also saw
the start of the craze for remakes, reboots
or reimaginings. The success of *The Texas
Chain Saw Massacre* – which added more
slasher movie trappings to the retelling
of the classic rural nightmare – ensured
that the craze would be long lasting. As
with most of these reboots and remakes, it
diluted the original's more extreme aspects

for maximum commercial appeal and lost some of the magic in the process. It was eventually followed by a prequel, *The Texas Chainsaw Massacre: The Beginning* (2006), which purports to show the genesis of Leatherface and his murderous clan. It garnered a reduced but still solid $39,517,763.

More inbred crazies populated *Wrong Turn* (2003), a violent, fast-paced, well-acted and exciting throwback to the backwoods horror typified by *Just Before Dawn* 20 years earlier. A group of young people are marooned in the forest of West Virginia and fall prey to a clan of cannibals. It did well enough to make $15,418,790 and almost matched that worldwide.

AN INFLUENTIAL GENRE

Murders in and around an exclusive school are not all they seem in the disappointing *Cry Wolf* (2005), which is so timid it almost seems embarrassed to be a slasher movie. Producers of the subgenre increasingly figured they could ring more money from younger filmgoers by going for the less-restrictive PG-13 rating. Not so afraid to revel in its absurdities is the remake of *House of Wax* (2005). The 1953 original was a forerunner to

DESMOND **HARRINGTON** ELIZA **DUSHKU** EMMANUELLE **CHRIQUI**

WRONG TURN

데드캠프

It's the last one you'll ever take.

SUMMIT ENTERTAINMENT AND CONSTANTIN FILM PRESENT DESMOND HARRINGTON ELIZA DUSHKU EMMANUELLE CHRIQUI JEREMY SISTO "WRONG TURN" AND KEVIN ZEGERS
MUSIC RANDY GERSTON EDITED ELIA CMIRAL STAN WINSTON STUDIO, INC. MICHAEL ROSS ALICIA KEYWAN JOHN S. BARTLEY, ASC, CSC
PATRICK WACHSBERGER MITCH HORWITS AARON RYDER DON CARMODY ROBERT KULZER ERIK FEIG STAN WINSTON BRIAN GILBERT ALAN McELROY ROB SCHMIDT

DVD VIDEO

Below and right Spanish poster artwork for *Cry Wolf* and American poster artwork for *Hatchet*.

Far right American promotional artwork for *Black Christmas*.

'VICTOR CROWLEY IS THE NEXT ICON OF HORROR.'
-HARRY KNOWLES. AIN'T IT COOL NEWS

HATCHET
OLD SCHOOL AMERICAN HORROR

WWW.HATCHETMOVIE.COM
STAY OUT OF THE SWAMP

the Golden Age slasher movie, but as was increasingly typical, this was a reimagining rather than a direct remake. It has more in common with the surreal 1970s slasher movie *Tourist Trap*, with six teenagers finding themselves hunted in a ghost town that houses a sinister wax museum. Raking in a respectable $32,064,800, it is most memorable for the crowd-pleasing moment when Paris Hilton is cut into itty-bitty pieces.

The year 2006 saw a veritable flurry of self-aware and nostalgic slasher movies. *Dark Ride* and *Hatchet* were both throwbacks to high-energy slashers in the early 1980s, using the settings of a theme park and swamp respectively. *Simon Says* and *The Tripper* were two of the stranger subgenre movies in recent years. In the former, the ever-watchable Crispin Glover (who got a machete to the face in *Friday the 13th: The Final Chapter* 22 years earlier) plays a twitchy backwoods psycho who makes

JUEGO MORTAL LLEGA AL INSTITUTO WESTLAKE

ITA SOSPECHAS
ANIPULA A TUS AMIGOS
IMINA TUS ENEMIGOS

CRY WOLF
ES UN INSTITUTO... NADA ES REAL.

convoluted traps for his human prey. *The Tripper* has a killer in a Ronald Reagan mask slicing his way through hippies at a festival. It was the main directorial feature début of *Scream* star David Arquette.

MAY ALL YOUR CHRISTMASES BE BLACK . . . AGAIN

This was also the year for eyeball plucking. Heavyweight WWE wrestling star Kane plays an orb-obsessed killer picking off teens in an abandoned hotel in *See No Evil*. Then came the remake of *Black Christmas* from Glen Morgan, the writer-producer of *Final Destination*

(2000). Perhaps wisely realizing he couldn't top the original, whose once-innovative aspects were now hoary old clichés, he takes the story of a sorority house full of girls being menaced by two killers on the eve of Christmas and turns it into a gleeful black comedy with moments of eye-popping suspense. Unfortunately, it didn't gel with audiences and made an unexceptional $16,273,581 domestically.

Still, *Black Christmas* fared better than *All the Boys Love Mandy Lane* (2006), where the lust for the eponymous girl turns deadly; it sat on the shelf unreleased in America for over three years, although it received theatrical and DVD releases overseas. Looking for another spin on the postmodernist slasher was the witty and intelligent *Behind the Mask: The Rise of Leslie Vernon* (2006), in which a documentary crew follow a fledgling serial killer who models himself on Freddy, Jason and Michael and reveals the tricks of his murderous trade. The belated sequel *I'll Always Know What You Did Last Summer* (2006) bypassed cinemas and was relegated to DVD release, all but ending that franchise (for the time being at least).

The most successful slasher of 2006 was, unsurprisingly, a remake. If there was one

This holiday season, the slay ride beg

BLACK X-MAS

criticism about the original *When a Stranger
Calls*, it was that, apart from starting and
ending with inspired suspense, the middle
section changed gears dramatically into a
police procedural drama. With the remake,
director Simon West aimed for all killer and
no filler by essentially stretching the first
15 minutes of the original over 87 minutes
with decidedly mediocre results. However,
it was a hit with younger audiences; it
was purposely made with a PG-13 rating
in mind, making a cool $47,860,214
domestically.

While *When a Stranger Calls* might have
been bland, no one could accuse Rob
Zombie's remake of *Halloween* of the same
crime. Unfortunately, that's pretty much
the only good thing you can say about
Halloween (2007). To paraphrase singer

Nick Cave, he said with cover versions you
need to get inside a song and destroy it
from the inside out; sometimes that works
and sometimes it doesn't. Musician Zombie
tried this approach with disastrous results,
systematically replacing everything that
made Carpenter's film so artful, graceful
and ultimately scary, as Haddonfield gets
invaded by trailer trash. Malcolm McDowell
as Dr. Loomis spends the entire film looking
like he wants to fire his agent, and who can
blame him? Evidently a love-it-or-hate-it
film, there were enough people who loved
it to scare up $58,272,029 domestically.
Zombie reportedly felt free of the constraints
of the original when making a sequel to his
remake, and *Halloween II* (2009) is more of
the same ultraviolence, only with ill-advised
surreal imagery. Audiences appeared to

have had enough of Zombie's vision, and the film made just over half of what the 2007 film did at the box office.

While the *Halloween* remake at least looked vibrant, the remake of *Prom Night* (2008) was the slasher equivalent of watching paint dry; it was so vapid and bland it was hardly even there. In essence, only the name was taken – the film finds a teenage girl stalked by a deranged ex-teacher, who kills her friends at a hotel on prom night. It is rather like the teenage TV series *The O.C.* with a body count, only not as scary. While the PG-13 rating prevented the inclusion of many of the elements that made Golden Age slasher movies so enjoyable, it did allow a young audience to drive this box-office success, with $43,869,350 in the bank. Diametrically

opposite to *Prom Night* was the small indie film *Murder Loves Killers Too* (2008), which showed that the slasher film could still surprise and thrill.

The remake juggernaut rolled into 2009 with somewhat better results. From Lionsgate, the makers of the *My Bloody Valentine* (2009) redux clearly knew what made the best early 1980s slashers tick. While it is never going to be great art, it is great fun – a bonus on the increasingly soulless remake conveyor belt. It didn't stick closely to the original, but it is at least sympathetic to it, with a homicidal miner wielding a pickaxe and again terrorizing a small mining town. To add to the roller-coaster, carnival feel of the film, it serves up impressively bloody special effects and does it all in 3D. The other bonus was that it generated enough interest to see the 1981 original released to DVD in all its uncut glory, which satisfied the calls of many fans over the years. Proving that both slasher

Below Remake bandwagon rolls on: promotional artwork for *Prom Night* (*left*) and *My Bloody Valentine* (*right*).

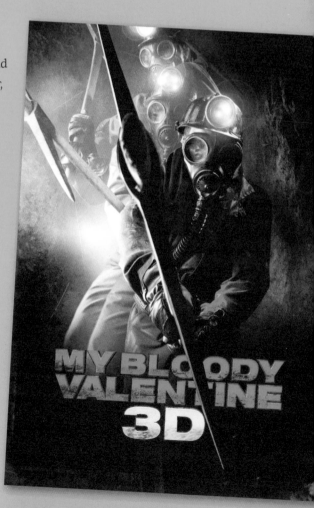

movies and 3D still had appeal, the remake made a healthy $51,545,952.

Friday the 13th (2009), ostensibly a redux of not only the first film but also the two immediate sequels, could never hope to do justice to all of them. The footage recapping the original film is over in the blink of an eye. In fact, the remake is curiously muted, despite its creators packing in enough violence, alcohol, drugs and sex for three films. However, America embraced the Sultan of Slaughter once again, shelling out $65,002,019.

ALL ABOARD THE REMAKE TRAIN

More reduxes appeared with the awful *Train* (2009), originally a remake of *Terror Train* that owes more to *Hostel* (2005). In the movie, American athletes are tortured at high speeds. *Sorority Row* (2009) is a remake of the 1983 slasher *The House on Sorority Row*. A fun throwback that makes the most of its entertainingly bitchy dialogue, it unfortunately peters out at the end. A female-driven movie, it surprisingly failed to find much of an audience, taking just $12 million at the domestic box office.

A new Freddy (Jackie Earle Haley) donned the fedora in the Michael Bay– produced *A Nightmare on Elm Street* (2010). Earning $63,075,011 in the United States, it was a financial success, if hardly one with fans and critics. Somehow the much anticipated *Scream 4* (2011) fared less well, despite reuniting director Wes Craven with the surviving original cast. It was curiously anaemic in both execution

and box-office clout, earning $38,180,928 domestically and failing to make back its budget – although it did better overseas. Further sequels in the *Friday the 13th* and *Halloween* franchises are certain, and *Child's Play* is next for the reboot treatment. Whether it's a remake, reboot or pretender to the throne, the slasher is unlikely to run out of blood anytime soon.

Far left and below Jason is back again in the 2009 remake of *Friday the 13th* (left); advance American promotional poster for *Sorority Row*.

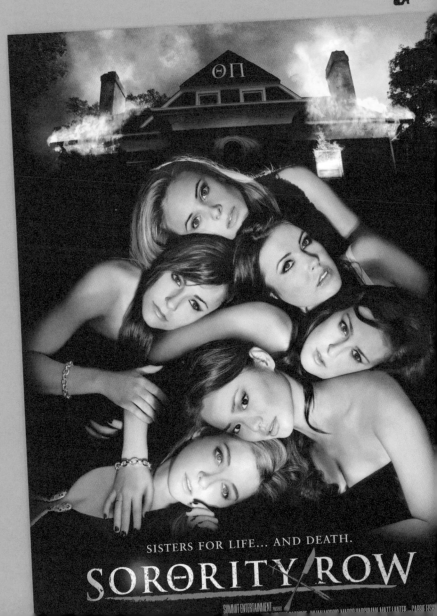

SISTERS FOR LIFE... AND DEATH.

SORORITY ROW

INTERNATIONAL SLASHING (1996 ONWARD)

Scream, and perhaps more so, I Know What You Did Last Summer, reignited interest in the subgenre around the world, although it took a little while for the boom to start.

Right Australian poster artwork for *Cut*.

ASIA

In Asia, Hong Kong's *The Deadly Camp* (*Shan gou 1999*, 1999) seems to take its inspiration from the backwoods slashers of the early 1980s. South Korea was especially prolific in kick-starting the trend with *Bloody Beach* (*Haebyeoneuro gada*, 2000), in which friends get murdered while on a beach vacation. *Nightmare* (*Gawi*, 2001) followed, mixing the supernatural chills of the phenomenally popular Japanese film *Ringu* (1998) with a typical slasher revenge angle. *The Record* (*Zzikhimyeon jukneunda*, 2001) was an entertaining and trashy variation of *I Know What You Did Last Summer*. *Bloody Reunion* (*Seuseung-ui eunhye*, 2006) somewhat predictably mixed the torture of *Hostel* with the subgenre, and Taiwan followed suit with *Invitation Only* (*Jue ming pai dui*, 2009).

Thailand's contributions to the subgenre are the back-jungle slasher *Scared* (*Rap nawng sayawng khwan*, 2005) and the manhunt thriller *Slice* (*Cheun*, 2009).

AUSTRALIA

Australia briefly returned to the genre, although without the gusto of the early 1980s, with the postmodern slasher *Cut* (2000). Its debt of gratitude to the Golden Age of the slasher came with casting Molly

Ringwald, who, although she had never made a horror movie before, is intrinsically linked to the 1980s through films such as *The Breakfast Club* (1985) and *Pretty in Pink* (1986).

INDIA

India produced what is perhaps the first-ever all-singing-all-dancing slasher movie with *Kucch To Hai* (2003). Another variation of *I Know What You Did Last Summer*, it quite shamelessly recreates whole sequences from that film, its sequel and *Urban Legend*. The same year's *Sssshhh . . .* continued Bollywood's magpie tendencies, taking *Scream* as its main inspiration. *Dhund: The Fog* (also 2003) followed with somewhat less delirious results.

EUROPE

Sweden contributed the awful and highly derivative *Camp Slaughter* (2004), which, perhaps unwisely, took its killer's bag-head look directly from Jason's fashion faux pas in the original *Friday the 13th Part 2*.

Just like in the early 1980s, the late 1990s slasher boom failed to resurrect the *giallo* in Italy in any significant way. Apart from Dario Argento's patchy returns to the art of the knife, perhaps most striking was Eros Puglielli's *Eyes of Crystal* (*Occhi di cristallo*, 2004). However, there was something of a renaissance in Britain, France and elsewhere in Europe. The British psycho-in-a-lighthouse opus *Lighthouse* (1999) was reminiscent of 1970s British shocker *Tower of Evil*.

Moving away from the satirical tone of *Scream*, British films that embraced the new wave of slasher included *Long Time Dead* (2002), *Creep* (2004), *The Descent* (2005), *Severance* (2006), *Wilderness* (2006), *Eden Lake* (2008), *The Children* (2008), and *Tormented* (2009). From France came two exceptionally visceral shockers, the excellent *High Tension* (*Haute tension*, 2003) and *Inside* (2007), the latter exploiting the fear of pregnant women that someone might want a baby so much she would kill for it. Austria's *Dead in 3 Days* (*In 3 Tagen bist du tot*, 2006) was a retelling of *I Know What You Did Last Summer*. The Netherlands produced *Slaughter Night* (*Sl8n8*, 2006), and Germany produced teen slashers *School's Out* (*Schrei–denn ich werde dich töten!*, 1999) and *The Pool* (*Swimming Pool – Der Tod feiert mit*, 2001). From Norway came *Cold Prey* (*Fritt Vilt*, 2006), featuring a psychopathic killer stalking hapless snowboarders in the snowy wastes; its sequel, *Cold Prey 2* (*Fritt Vilt II*, 2008), is one of the best post-*Scream* slashers of recent years.

Below American video artwork for *School's Out*.

SCHOOL'S OUT

This Class Is Dying To Graduate.

CONCLUSION

The end? I don't think so. As much as it's loathed and loved in equal measures, and as long as it remains profitable, the slasher subgenre is sure to survive. There will always be nostalgia for these movies, and today's teenagers will look back fondly on the slasher films of today (even if they are mostly pale imitations).

The slasher film's story is a strange one, to be sure. Developing from its unlikely roots at Le Théâtre du Grand Guignol by way of Agatha Christie and the 'Old Dark House' thrillers of the 1920s and 1930s, it started to take the form we recognize today with the release of *Psycho* and the films that followed in its wake, spinning off into the glorious international hybrids of the *krimi* and *giallo*.

RULING THE BOX OFFICE

Proto-slashers such as *Black Christmas* and *The Texas Chain Saw Massacre* provided the impetus for the birth of the seminal modern slasher, *Halloween*, in 1978. It launched a new horror movement that all but ruled the box office in the early 1980s, with *Friday the 13th* and a hundred others leading the bloody onslaught. The slasher has shown its staying power by riding out the tough times, during which it became unfashionable and descended into low-budget video hell.

The slasher rebirth in 1996 showed that you can't keep a good subgenre down. It is remarkable that it survived being spoofed and deconstructed only to flourish again

with a straight face. Today, in the era of genre reboots, the mighty box office of many remakes of subgenre classics – such as *Friday the 13th* and *Prom Night* – show that despite their failings, these films still demand our attention.

The slasher has courted controversy in the past. At first dismissed by mainstream critics as unworthy of scrutiny, the subgenre crossed into the mainstream with a vengeance in the late 1970s and early 1980s and could no longer be ignored by its detractors. Its critics over the years have been legion – from the government and censors to film critics and women's and gay rights groups – but the slasher film has weathered every storm.

IMPERVIOUS TO CRITICISM

Much to the displeasure of its detractors, the subgenre is mostly impervious to bad reviews and other brickbats. And, while continuing to cannibalize its past, the slasher movie still has the power to surprise, unnerve and shock, with films such the recent French example *Inside* (*À l'intérieur*, 2007), which rips its story from today's tabloids.

A killer waits at the high school dance.

If you're not back by midnight... you won't be coming home!

A SIMCOM PRODUCTION
LESLIE NIELSEN · JAMIE LEE CURTIS IN "PROM NIGHT"
SCREENPLAY BY WILLIAM GRAY · STORY BY ROBERT GUZA, JR.
PRODUCED BY PETER SIMPSON · DIRECTED BY PAUL LYNCH

PROM NIGHT

AN AVCO EMBASSY PICTURE
Released by BARBER ROSE INTERNATIONAL FILMS LTD.

x

BREEDING TALENT

The slasher has also been a fertile breeding ground for today's talent. It is arguable whether directors John Carpenter or Wes Craven would even have careers today if it weren't for their part in the history of the subgenre. Many young stars of film and TV owe the subgenre a nod of gratitude in helping them up the career ladder. Again, it's debatable whether the careers of film celebrities such as Johnny Depp, Daryl Hannah and Tom Hanks would have blossomed the way they have if they hadn't had early roles in slasher movies. Whether it likes it or not, Hollywood also owes a lot to the slasher movie for some of its best off-screen talent, such as the cinematographer Dean Cundey, who was much praised for his work on *Halloween*, and composer Ennio Morricone for his excellent *giallo* work.

There will always be fresh blood, as every new generation of teenagers stumbles across its own forgotten campground or abandoned mineshaft or creepy carnival with a long-buried secret, and there will always be an audience to cheer on their inevitable demise. The subgenre will inevitably go from the marquee to the bargain bin and back again, but one thing's for sure, the slasher movie is the celluloid equivalent of its protagonists Freddy, Jason and Michael – it will simply never die.

Above The homecoming queen won't be coming home: British cinema artwork for the original *Prom Night*.

GOLDEN AGE SLASHER REVIEWS

This section features 10 of the key films of the Golden Age chosen as some of the best examples of the subgenre. The reviews are condensed versions of those on my site, Hysterial Lives! (www.hysteria-lives.co.uk), and the synopses are brief, as the films have already been mentioned in the main text.

Each listing features the title and year, main credits, choice dialogue, synopsis and review.

Key:
d – director
p – producer
c – cast

FRIDAY THE 13TH (1980)

Georgetown Productions Inc./Paramount Pictures; United States; 95 minutes
d Sean S. Cunningham
p Sean S. Cunningham
c Betsy Palmer, Adrienne King, Jeannine Taylor, Robbi Morgan, Kevin Bacon

Choice dialogue: 'Do ya think you'll last all summer?'
'I don't know if I'm going to last all week!'

Synopsis: In 1958 a tragic accident at Camp Crystal Lake sees the supposed drowning of a young boy while camp counsellors are too busy making out to hear his cries. Later, following a fireside sing-a-long, an unseen assailant murders two of the counsellors. The summer camp is quickly closed. In 1980 a plucky young bunch of people are hired to prepare the camp before the summer season, despite the dire warnings that they are 'all doomed!' One by one, they begin to fall victim to an unseen killer.

Review: It's hard to remember that, before *Friday the 13th*, summer camps were synonymous with the innocence of childhood and not the slaughter of the nubile. Like *Halloween*, *Friday the 13th* takes a place of previous safety and effectively turns it into a charnel house. It's also hard to imagine a time before unstoppable killing machine Jason Voorhees (though minus a precredits shock, he doesn't turn up until the sequel). In an inverse of *Psycho*, the villain of the piece is his mother (Palmer), veering wildly between the maternal and psychotic. It is she – with her teeth like tombstones – who helps make *Friday the 13th* such an increasingly campy pleasure. The iconic soundtrack by Harry Manfredini adds to the ghoulish glee. Of course, the real stars of the film are Tom Savini's still-remarkable gore effects. A face is smashed with an axe; a throat is punctured with an arrow in loving, bubbling close-up. It was catapulting this level of gratuitous violence from the grindhouse to the mainstream that secured a box-office bonanza.

Ultimately, taking its lead from *Halloween* and Bava's *Bay of Blood*, *Friday the 13th* takes Agatha Christie's *Ten Little Indians* to its logical conclusion.

PROM NIGHT (1980)

Prom Night Productions; Canada; 90 minutes
d Paul Lynch
p Peter Simpson
c Leslie Nielsen, Jamie Lee Curtis, Casey Stevens, Anne-Marie Martin, Antoinette Bower

Choice dialogue: 'Psychotic! . . . Disfigured! . . . Violent! . . . He has to be hiding somewhere . . . waiting. I gotta get that bastard before he butchers someone else!'

Synopsis: A group of children play a game whereby they stalk a younger child, but she accidentally falls to her death. They try to cover their tracks, but someone saw what they did. Six years later, the friends prepare for their prom. Meanwhile, the wrongfully accused chief suspect for the girl's murder has escaped from the asylum, and police fear he may be coming back to town. As the teens get ready to take to the dance floor, someone in a balaclava is looking for retribution.

Review: Director Paul Lynch exploits cliché after cliché to the point of near parody. Practically every element of the burgeoning teens-in-peril subgenre is present: the threatening phone calls from *When a Stranger Calls*, the sins of the past revisiting the future, a creepy red-herring handyman. The escaped lunatic from an asylum has always been a cliché, but here it gives more than a nod to Carpenter's *Halloween*. And, of course, the filmmaker's major coup was signing that film's star.

Unfortunately, *Prom Night* is woefully lacking the suspense of *Halloween* and is mired by murky lighting. Thankfully, Curtis gives a bravura performance in the face of ineptitude and indifference. However, *Prom Night* is difficult not to like precisely because of its failings. Where the film excels is in camp and cheese. After indulging in premarital sex and drugs, one girl coos, 'I'll remember this night for the rest of my life!' just before being offed by the killer. One of the main selling points of the film at the time were the scenes featuring disco dancing, which was then in vogue. The film's notable moment is when a severed head rolls along the prom catwalk, causing widespread panic amongst the disco bunnies.

TERROR TRAIN (1980)

Triple T Productions; Canada; 97 minutes
d Roger Spottiswoode
p Harold Greenberg
c Ben Johnson, Jamie Lee Curtis,

Hart Bochner, David Copperfield,
Derek McKinnon, Sandee Currie

Choice dialogue: 'With a party like that
I'm always afraid some kid's going to hurt
themselves.'

Synopsis: Students arrange a graduation
celebration on a train, and·along for the
ride are a magician and his mysterious
female assistant. However, also along for
the ride is someone with murder on his/
her mind, and the student body begins to
be whittled down one by one.

Review: Of course *Terror Train* is famous
for being another of the slasher films that
Curtis made after *Halloween*. Here she is
a little bit more cocky but is essentially
still a sympathetic character; battling the
psycho and doing Final Girl duty. Despite
an arresting opening, the film drags in the
first half. The makers seemed so thrilled to
have real-life magician David Copperfield's
involvement that they forgot to get the
film moving. Thankfully the killer, who
wears the costume of the last person killed,
actually looks pretty spooky, with cold
eyes peering emotionless from behind
the succession of masks stolen from each
victim in turn.

Terror Train is surprisingly sadistic,
especially towards the end when the tone
changes quite dramatically from cheesy
to something a few shades darker. You get
the sense that whoever is doing the killing
really wants to make the group suffer – and
as the group is mostly male, they make
up most of the film's victims (only one

victim is female). Curtis shines during the
climactic confrontation with the killer,
with Spottiswoode making good use of the
claustrophobic train setting. The film is
blessed with a strong performance from
Bochner as a nasty frat boy and striking
cinematography by John Alcott (who did
The Shining that same year). The final twist
is silly but satisfying.

THE BURNING (1981)

Filmways Pictures/The Cropsy Venture;
United States); 91 minutes
d Tony Maylam
p Harvey Weinstein
c Brian Matthews, Leah Ayres,
  Brian Backer, Larry Joshua,
  Jason Alexander, Ned Eisenberg,
  Fisher Stevens, Lou David, Holly Hunter

Choice dialogue: 'He's out there watching
. . . waiting. So don't look – he'll see you.
Don't breathe – he'll hear you. Don't move
. . . YOU'RE DEAD!'

Synopsis: A much-hated caretaker at
Camp Blackfoot summer camp, nicknamed
Cropsy, is horribly burned when the
kids decide to play a trick on him – with
tragic consequences. Leaving the hospital,
garden shears in hand, Cropsy returns to
his old stomping ground to do a little teen
pruning.

Review: Perhaps the most obvious rip off of
(or homage to, if you're feeling generous)
the previous year's *Friday the 13th*, *The
Burning* remains infamous for the level

of gory screen violence orchestrated by special-effects maestro Tom Savini – he turned down *Friday the 13th Part 2* to work on this film. It was violent enough to earn 'video nasty' status in Britain.

Cropsy is an expert with the shears and sends fingers flying; he literally cuts the population of the camp down to size. Most notable is a bravura set piece where he hides inside a canoe and jumps out to kill a group of teenagers in quick succession.

Perhaps buoyed by the success of summer-camp comedies such as *Meatballs* (1979), *The Burning* suffers from spending too much time on the would-be comedic pratfalls and pranks of the young cast. However, Cropsy is an iconic and threatening presence with his shears and vengeful silence. The Rick Wakeman score is annoyingly insistent.

Although it never gave birth to a sequel, the film was the launchpad of several of today's stars, including Jason Alexander (of *Seinfeld*) and Academy Award–winning actress Holly Hunter in a blink-and-you'll-miss-it part. The film also has the distinction of being one of the few early 1980s slashers to feature a Final Boy rather than a Final Girl.

THE FUNHOUSE (1981)

Mace Neufeld Productions/Universal Pictures; United States; 96 minutes
d Tobe Hooper
p Steven Bernhardt and Derek Power
c Elizabeth Berridge, Shawn Carson, Jeanne Austin, Jack McDermott, Cooper Huckabee, Largo Woodruff, Miles Chapin, Kevin Conway, Wayne Doba

Choice dialogue: 'There will be no escape . . . for there is no release from the funhouse!'

Synopsis: At the fairground Amy (Berridge) and three teenage friends get off the ghost train in the funhouse to spend the night there. However, they accidentally spy one of the carnival hands in a Frankenstein mask killing the fortune-teller after she laughs at his sexual inadequacy. They find themselves trapped with what is revealed to be a hideously deformed albino who hunts them down one by one.

Review: Horror star Lon Chaney once said, 'A clown is funny in the circus ring, but what would be the normal reaction to opening a door at midnight and finding the same clown standing there in the moonlight?' Hooper's film uses this juxtaposition of carefree merriment and creeping terror with a small degree of success in *The Funhouse*.

Both *Halloween* and *Psycho* are parodied in the film's opening scene when Amy is attacked in the shower by a mask-wearing assailant. Mirroring what was to come, the would-be killer turns out to be her little brother playing a prank. The film also harkens back to classic horror movies – not surprising given Universal's involvement.

The killer is pitiful if not exactly sympathetic, a nod to Universal's original monster of Frankenstein. Unfortunately, the film's protagonists are not especially sympathetic either. Also, Hooper seems less interested in the setup for the mayhem that is about to ensue and more interested in cataloguing the weird and sinister people at the carnival. For no good reason, *The Funhouse* ended up for a while as a 'video nasty' in Britain, despite being one of the least gory slasher flicks of the time.

HAPPY BIRTHDAY TO ME (1981)

Canadian Film Development Corporation (CFDC)/Columbia Pictures Corporation/ Famous Players/The Birthday Film Company; Canada; 110 minutes
d J. Lee Thompson
p John Dunning and André Link
c Melissa Sue Anderson, Glenn Ford, Tracey E. Bregman, Matt Craven, Lenore Zann, Lisa Langlois, Lesleh Donaldson

Choice dialogue: 'Maybe we should all put in $20 and the last one left takes all!'
Synopsis: Just before Virginia's 18th birthday, someone wearing black leather gloves is killing the self-elected 'Top 10' at the Crawford Academy. Virginia suffers from alarming blackouts, and increasingly the finger of suspicion points at her. Could she be behind the killings? Or is it something to do with a freak accident in her past that left her needing brain surgery and her mother dead? And will she find out before it comes time to sing 'Happy Birthday to Me'?

Review: Thompson had directed the well-regarded psycho-thriller *Cape Fear* (1962), so some may have seen helming a gory little Canadian teen shocker as a step down. Not me! *Happy Birthday to Me* is fun with a capital F.

It is perhaps the best example of the early 1980s teen slasher movie that recognizes its absurdities and embraces them with vigour. If any slasher movie from this time comes close to capturing the joyful delirium of an episode of *Scooby Doo*, it is this one–no more so than during the closing 15 minutes, when the deceased are placed ghoulishly around a table for Virginia's birthday celebration. This culminates in an outlandish, grand unmasking and bittersweet ending that has to be seen to be believed.

Using this film to break away from the wholesome image she had in the TV show *Little House on the Prairie*, Anderson convinces and keeps a straight face as the much-beleaguered Virginia.

As with *Friday the 13th*, the true stars are the murders, with the publicity making much of the fact that audiences were invited to witness 'six of the most bizarre murders that you will ever see', including an Isadora Duncan–inspired death by scarf in a motorbike wheel, death by weight-lifting aparatus, and, most infamously, death by shish kebab! We'll gloss over the fact that there are actually nine deaths in this movie and not six.

It is one of the longest slasher movies ever made, clocking in at 110 minutes.

HELL NIGHT (1981)

BLT Productions/Media Home
Entertainment; United States; 101 minutes
d Tom DeSimone
p Irwin Yablans and Bruce Cohn Curtis
c Linda Blair, Vincent Van Patten,
    Peter Barton, Kevin Brophy,
    Jenny Neumann, Suki Goodwin

Choice dialogue: 'If you weren't screaming,
and we weren't screaming – then someone
is trying to mind-fuck us here!'

Synopsis: Desperate to join the Alpha
Sigma Rho fraternity and its sister sorority,
four pledges must prove themselves by
staying the night in a supposedly haunted
house. That night, a murderous presence
stirs and is none too pleased that a bunch
of boozing, pill-popping, sex-crazed teens
are trespassing!

Review: In the first few frames the
screaming mouth of a teenage girl fills the
screen. This isn't a scream of real terror
but a fog-horn howl to signal the ghoulish
campery has begun. *Hell Night* is a good-
times ghost train of a slasher movie:
hokey and creaky, but always fun. The
spooky gothic mansion makes the perfect
backdrop, and decking out the teenagers in
costumes nicely reinforces the funhouse
feel. The film's bogeymen do their jobs
with relish, and the whole cast is clearly
having a blast throughout.

Blair plays Marti, who is earmarked
as the Final Girl not just because of her
star status but from her boyish name, à la
Jamie Lee Curtis's Laurie in *Halloween*.

Relatively light on blood and nudity, it is
still one of the most enjoyable of the early
1980s slasher flicks. It takes itself seriously
enough to stop from descending into farce
and positively revels in its absurdities.
Director DeSimone handles the action
well, apart from an ill-advised detour into
the supernatural.

Although it seems funny to talk about
innocence in a film where a bunch of
people are carved up in creative ways, *Hell
Night* is a perfect twilight example of the
slasher flick before it descended into self-
parody and saw its budgets shrink.

MY BLOODY VALENTINE (1981)

Secret Films/Canadian Film Development
Corporation/Famous Players; Canada; 91
minutes
d George Mihalka
p André Link, John Dunning,
    Stephen Miller
c Paul Kelman, Lori Hallier, Neil Affleck,
    Keith Knight, Alf Humphreys,
    Cynthia Dale, Helene Udy, Rob Stein,
    Thomas Kovacs, Peter Cowper

Choice dialogue: 'You gotta see the dress
I got. Cut down to there, split up to here
. . . I may not get out alive!'

Synopsis: Twenty years ago the small
town of Valentine Bluffs was rocked by
an explosion in the Hanniger Coal Mines.
Harry Warden (Cowper), the only survivor,
took bloody revenge on the supervisors
who neglected their duties while partying
at the annual Valentine's Day dance. He

left a chilling warning never to hold the dance again. Now, 20 years later, that warning is ignored as the town gears up to celebrate Valentine's Day once more.

Review: A hugely enjoyable, well-acted piece of Canadian slasher hokum. *My Bloody Valentine* has a high-sheen gloss, above-average production values and crisp cinematography.

The mad miner is one of the subgenre's best and most iconic villains: silent and menacing in his gas mask, carrying a pick axe and ready for mayhem. The setting is used to great effect as the victims-to-be try to find their way up from the confusing maze of mine tunnels; one is never quite sure what lurks behind a darkened corner or what hides in the shadows.

The film also manages a good few popcorn jolts, as well as being genuinely frightening in places, especially when the killer walks slowly in pursuit, smashing each light bulb, plunging more of the mine into total blackness. However, choppy editing originally hurt the film, which was the fault of overzealous censors demanding the film be shorn of its most explicit elements. Overall, it's one of the best slashers movies from the early 1980s.

THE HOUSE ON SORORITY ROW (1983)

(aka *House of Evil*)
Artists Releasing Corporation (ARC)/Film Ventures International (FVI)/VAE; United States; 91 minutes
d Mark Rosman
p John G. Clark, Mark Rosman

c Kate McNeil, Eileen Davidson, Janis Ward, Robin Meloy, Harley Jane Kozak, Jodi Draigie, Ellen Dorsher, Lois Kelso Hunt

Choice dialogue: 'One good old-fashioned sorority prank!'

Synopsis: In a prologue, Mrs. Slater (Hunt) gives birth to a deformed baby. Some 22 years later she has turned her home into a sorority house, which is now closing for the holidays. Everyone is leaving, apart from a group of seven girls planning a party that weekend. Slater refuses to let the party take place and further angers the girls by slashing one of their waterbeds with the sharp-tipped walking cane she carries everywhere. Furious, they plan a prank to pay her back.

It goes tragically wrong when Slater is accidentally killed. Panicking, the girls sink her body to the bottom of a swimming pool. For appearance's sake and to avoid suspicion, the party is held. To the girls' horror, the body vanishes, and while the party continues to swing, they begin to meet grisly ends at the hands of someone carrying the housemother's lethal cane.

Review: One of the best slasher movies of the subgenre surprisingly came towards the end of the Golden Age. Director Rosman is blessed with a likable and generally talented cast, especially McNeil, who is great as the movie's Final Girl. Only Hunt's stiff turn as Slater jars, while, perhaps ironically, Draigie's heroically awful performance as one of the girls only adds to the fun. Cleverly plotted and bolstered by a good score from genre regular Richard Band, there is an intriguing subplot and enough twists and turns to keep the most jaded slasher fan on their toes. Brian De Palma protégé Rosman shows a flair for the macabre: a head turns up in the toilet bowl, children's toys appear before many of the murders, the killer's clown costume is extremely creepy, and, in an especially effective scene, McNeil discovers all her friends floating dead in the swimming pool. The party (complete with de rigeur bad 1980s band) lends a pleasingly cheesy feel to the proceedings but doesn't overpower the horror and thriller elements.

A NIGHTMARE ON ELM STREET (1984)

(New Line Cinema/Smart Egg Pictures; United States; 91 minutes

d Wes Craven

p Robert Shaye, Sara Risher

c John Saxon, Ronee Blakley, Heather Langenkamp, Amanda Wyss, Jsu Garcia, Johnny Depp, Robert Englund

Choice dialogue: 'Whatever you do, don't fall asleep.'

Synopsis: Four high school students discover they are having similar nightmares about a bogeyman figure in a dirty red-and-green-striped sweater stalking them. On his right hand is a glove with knives as fingers. They begin to die one by one in seemingly impossible ways. Nancy (Langenkamp) finds out the strange events may be linked to a child killer who died in a fire years before. She discovers that dreams really can kill and does everything she can to stay awake.

Review: *A Nightmare on Elm Street* introduced Freddy Krueger (Englund) to the world – it was also my introduction to the slasher cinema-going experience.

Masterfully helmed by genre regular Wes Craven, it was a breath of fresh air for the subgenre. Surreal and genuinely unnerving, it uses the basic setup for the teen slasher flick but takes it in new directions. Craven understands the way that dreams and nightmares work – the fuzzy logic of not questioning how a step through a doorway can lead you somewhere you shouldn't be.

There are also creepily effective, off-kilter flourishes (the sheep running along a school corridor; the bloody living corpse in the body bag). Many of the later sequels turned Freddy into a cartoonish buffoon, and it's easy to forget that he was a genuinely frightening presence in the original. Langenkamp plays what could be seen as the ultimate Final Girl. Almost a pastiche of the heroines in other slasher movies, she is limitlessly resourceful, plotting and setting booby traps for her climactic battle with Freddy, who really meets his match. The young cast, including a fresh-faced Johnny Depp, acquit themselves well, but an appalling turn by Ronee Blakley as Nancy's mother provides some laughs but detracts from what is otherwise a first-rate chiller.

THE TOP 10 BODY COUNTS

HALLOWEEN

BODY COUNT 5 ✝✝✝✝✝
Female: 3 Male: 2

1. Female repeatedly stabbed with butcher's knife
2. Male's corpse glimpsed in undergrowth
3. Female strangled and stabbed
4. Male impaled on butcher's knife
5. Female strangled with telephone cord

FRIDAY THE 13TH

BODY COUNT 9 ✝✝✝✝✝✝✝✝✝
Female: 4 Male: 5

1. Male stabbed in gut
2. Female has throat slit (off-screen)
3. Female has throat slit
4. Male has throat slit (off-screen)
5. Male has arrow forced through neck
6. Female has axe buried in her face
7. Female killed (method unseen)
8. Male stabbed in gut
9. Male has throat slit; shot with arrows (off-screen)
10. Female decapitated with machete

PROM NIGHT

BODY COUNT 8 ✝✝✝✝✝✝✝✝
Female: 5 Male: 3

1. Young girl falls to her death after prank backfires
2. Female found stabbed to death with broken glass (off-screen)
3. Female has throat slit with shard of glass
4. Female stabbed to death with shard of glass
5. Male dies when van goes over a cliff and explodes
6. Female killed with axe
7. Male decapitated with axe
8. Male dies from head wound inflicted with axe

THE BURNING

BODY COUNT 10 ✝✝✝✝✝✝✝✝✝✝
Female: 5 Male: 5

1. Female stabbed with scissors and pushed through window
2. Female has throat cut with garden shears
3. Male stabbed in the chest with shears

4. Female stabbed in the stomach with shears
5. Male has his fingers snipped off with shears
6. Male stabbed in the neck with shears
7. Female slashed across the forehead with shears
8. Female teen stabbed with shears (off-screen)
9. Male teen impaled on shears (through neck)
10. Male impaled on shears, head split with axe and then set on fire

THE FUNHOUSE

BODY COUNT 6 ††††††
Female: 2 Male: 4
1. Female strangled
2. Male hanged and then gets an axe to the head
3. Female strangled and bludgeoned to death
4. Male impaled on sword
5. Male shot dead
6. Male crushed to death in the funhouse machinery

HAPPY BIRTHDAY TO ME

BODY COUNT 9 †††††††††
Female: 3 Male: 6
1. Female has throat cut with 'cut-throat' razor
2. Male's face is dragged into motorcycle wheel after his scarf is thrown into it
3. Male crushed by weight-lifting apparatus
4. Male stabbed in gut with garden shears
5. Male impaled on shish kebab through mouth
6. Female drowns when car goes into river
7. Male battered to death with poker
8. Male has throat slit
9. Female stabbed in gut with knife

HELL NIGHT

BODY COUNT 8 ††††††††
Female: 2 Male: 6
1. Female decapitated with machete
2. Male has neck broken
3. Male impaled on scythe
4. Male shot with shotgun
5. Male killed (method unseen)
6. Female body found
7. Male thrown to his death
8. Male impaled on gate spikes

MY BLOODY VALENTINE

BODY COUNT 12 ††††††††††††
Female: 5 Male: 7

1. Female impaled on spike
2/3. Two males pickaxed to death (one unseen) and hearts removed
4. Female pickaxed and then tumble dried to death
5. Male pickaxed through chest
6. Male has face pushed into pot of boiling water
7. Female impaled on shower unit
8/9. Male and female impaled by industrial drill while having sex
10. Male shot with nail gun in head
11. Male hung and then decapitated
12. Female pickaxed through stomach

HOUSE ON SORORITY ROW

BODY COUNT 9 †††††††††
Female: 7 Male: 2

1. Female shot dead
2. Male given bloody tracheotomy with walking cane
3. Female stabbed to death with cane
4. Female impaled on cane
5. Female has hand impaled and then stabbed to death with cane
6. Female decapitated with knife
7. Female has throat cut
8. Female hacked to death with cane
9. Male hacked to death with cane

A NIGHTMARE ON ELM STREET

BODY COUNT 4 ††††
Female: 2 Male: 2

1. Female slashed to death
2. Male hung on twisted sheets
3. Male pulled through bed and liquidized
4. Female burnt to death

BEFORE THEY WERE FAMOUS

Apart from Jamie Lee Curtis, a number of today's screen celebrities also started out in slasher movies during the subgenre's Golden Age, although many may choose to forget it.

Holly Hunter: The Oscar winner's first film role was as a teen camper in a blink-and-you'll-miss-it part in *The Burning* (1981).

Jason Alexander: Another *The Burning* survivor making his début was the TV funny man most famous for his role in the popular TV comedy series *Seinfeld*.

Kevin Bacon: Played the consummate horny teenager in the original *Friday the 13th* (1980). He is still making high-profile films in Hollywood today.

Johnny Depp: Played the Final Girl's love interest in *A Nightmare on Elm Street* (1984).

Kevin Costner: *The Untouchables* (1987) star made his début in the terminally cheesy slasher *Shadows Run Black* (1981).

Dennis Quaid: Had an early role as a love interest in TV slasher *Are You in the House Alone?* (1978).

Daryl Hannah: Battled a psychotic forest woman in *The Final Terror* (1983). She didn't die but did have her throat slashed and sewn back up in the movie.

Jennifer Jason Leigh: Played a deaf, mute and blind teenager who fights back against the mad killer in *Eyes of a Stranger* (1980).

Rachel Ward: Fought for her life in *The Final Terror*. However, she was also a suspect for the decapitation murders in *Night School* (1981).

Brooke Shields: *Communion* (1976) saw Shields make her film début as a child who is strangled just ahead of her first holy communion.

Christopher Lloyd: Before the *Back to the Future* film series (1985–1990) cemented his fame, Lloyd played the archetypal creepy boiler man in *Schizoid* (1980).

Tom Hanks: Made his movie début in *He Knows You're Alone* (1980) as a good-natured psychology major called Elliott who escapes the killer's knife.

And others: The end of the Golden Age of slasher movies didn't stop eager young actors and actresses from lining up to appear in them. A few more include Kristin Davis (of *Sex and the City* fame), who had her face cut in half with a buzz saw in *Doom Asylum* (1987); Brad Pitt survived having his head put in a vice in *Cutting Class* (1989); Jennifer Aniston was chased by a tiny but deadly Irishman in *Leprechaun* (1993); and Renée Zellweger and Matthew McConaughey slummed it in *Return of the Texas Chainsaw Massacre* (1994).

BLOODBATH AT THE BOX OFFICE

Below is a selection of Golden Age slashers that lit up the box office (and some that didn't). Listed are the original box-office takings in the United States as well as those adjusted for inflation. To put it in perspective, when adjusted, John Carpenter's *Halloween* made more than twice as much money as the 2007 remake.

TITLE	YEAR	ORIGINAL TAKE	ADJUSTED FOR INFLATION
Halloween	1978	$47,000,000	$144,213,675
When a Stranger Calls	1979	$20,149,106	$57,637,681
Friday the 13th	1980	$39,754,601	$121,982,066
He Knows You're Alone	1980	$4,875,436	$13,013,245
Prom Night	1980	$14,796,236	$39,493,298
Silent Scream	1980	$15,800,000	$42,172,490
Eyes of a Stranger	1981	$1,118,634	$2,889,133
Friday the 13th Part 2	1981	$21,722,776	$56,104,148
Halloween II	1981	$25,533,818	$65,947,054
Happy Birthday to Me	1981	$10,000,000	$25,827,338
Hell Night	1981	$2,300,000	$5,940,287
My Bloody Valentine	1981	$5,672,031	$14,649,346
Friday the 13th Part 3	1982	$34,581,519	$84,454,182
Visiting Hours	1982	$13,258,670	$32,380,017
The House on Sorority Row	1983	$10,604,986	$24,172,634
Psycho II	1983	$34,725,000	$79,150,948
A Nightmare on Elm Street	1984	$25,504,513	$54,500,714
Friday the 13th: The Final Chapter	1984	$32,980,880	$70,476,998
Silent Night, Deadly Night	1984	$2,491,460	$5,324,012

Figures taken from Boxofficemojo.com and the-numbers.com.

GLOSSARY

body count: Describes the methodology and the number of murders. Typically, the murders themselves are the true stars of the movie, and the plot is often used merely to link them together. Some slasher films – namely the *Friday the 13th* series – utilized the body count as a way of selling the picture, featuring it heavily in the series' cinema trailers.

creative kill: Makers of slasher films tried to outdo each other when it came to killing off their young casts in novel ways, vying to be even more outlandish than before. Creative kills included everything from death by electric guitar (*Home Sweet Home*) to murder by microwave oven (*Evil Laugh*).

Final Girl (FG): A resourceful woman or teenage girl who fights back against the murderer and lives to the end of the film, while her friends have been picked off one by one.

Grand Guignol: Takes its name from the Parisian Théâtre du Grand Guignol (the Theatre of the Big Puppet), which opened in 1897 and specialized in naturalistic horror plays. Today, the name is still used as a general term for graphic horror entertainment.

giallo: An Italian genre of film that was popular in the 1960s and 1970s in Italy. Its origins are in lurid paperback thrillers with yellow covers (*giallo* means 'yellow' in Italian). *Gialli* typically feature a series of violent murders performed by a villain whose identity is kept hidden until the conclusion.

killer: Without someone behind the mayhem there would be no slasher movie. Often masked, disfigured and invariably deranged, the killer's objective is to creatively dispatch as many as possible. Bad, mad and certainly dangerous to know, the killer in the slasher film is usually, though not always, a man. In many slasher films, especially later ones, the killer often takes on seemingly supernatural powers of regeneration.

krimi: This term simply translates as 'crime'. These films were popular German adaptations in the late 1950s and 1960s of the stories by British writer Edgar Wallace (and later his son Bryan Edgar Wallace). They are typically set in England, featuring a murderous villain in often outlandish disguises and a corresponding police investigation.

They influenced the *giallo*, then the slasher movie.

POV (point of view): A subjective camera angle that shows the action from the eyes of the killer to put the audience in the killer's place. It is a popular device used in slasher movies to disguise the identity of the killer or to scare the audience.

proto-slasher: Films that typically employ some of the conventions of the slasher movie (such as the POV shot or Final Girl, for example). However, they predate *Halloween* and the slasher films that followed it and, while sharing some aspects, do not always conform to the slasher movie's formula and have more in common with the psycho-thriller. Proto-slashers are forerunners of the slasher movie.

psycho-thriller: Similar to the slasher movie, these tend to be mainstream films that employ slasher conventions to accentuate the on-screen action but not form its main basis.

slasher movie: A film where, typically, a group of people (often teenagers) are targeted by a killer and are killed off one by one. The murders are often flamboyantly gory and invariably feature sharp implements such as knives or power tools. The slasher film typically employs cat-and-mouse suspense and special effects to frighten and entertain audiences. The first modern movie considered to be a slasher was John Carpenter's iconic *Halloween* (1978). Also known as *stalk 'n' slash*, *slice 'n' dice* or *dead teenager movie*.

slasher sequels: The slasher movie, of all subgenres, arguably generated more sequels than any other. Often, these are a variation on the same story – although often with a twist, such as sending the villain and victims into space (for example, *Jason X*). Slasher sequels (or *franchises*, as they are sometimes called), are driven by box-office success rather than critical acclaim.

splatter movie (or gore movie): These differ from the slasher movie in that they are mostly concerned with showing violent and gory acts on-screen in an over-the-top manner.

T&A: Stands for 'tits and ass'. Nudity was the ying to the slasher movie's violence yang. Many slasher movies complemented the on-screen mayhem with flashes of bare flesh (sometimes male but mostly female) to titillate audiences.

FURTHER READING AND WEBSITES

BOOKS

Brewster, Francis, Harvey Fenton, and Marc Morris. *Shock! Horror! Astounding Artwork from the Video Nasty Era*. London: FAB Press, 2005.

Chibnall, Steve. *Making Mischief: The Cult Films of Pete Walker*. London: FAB Press, 1998.

Clover, Carol J. *Men, Women, and Chain Saws: Gender in the Modern Horror Film*. Princeton, NJ: Princeton University Press, 1993.

Fenton, Harvey, and David Flint, eds. *Ten Years of Terror: British Horror Films of the 1970s*. London: FAB Press, 2001.

Hardy, Phil, ed. *The Overlook Film Encyclopedia: Science Fiction*. New York: Overlook Press, 1995.

Harper, Jim. *Legacy of Blood: A Comprehensive Guide to Slasher Movies*. London: Headpress/Critical Vision, 2004.

Kerekes, David, and David Slater. *See No Evil: Banned Films and Video Controversy*. London: Headpress/ Critical Vision, 2000.

Martin, John. *The Seduction of the Gullible: The Curious History of the British "Video Nasties" Phenomenon*. 2nd ed. Milwaukee, WI: Procrustes Press, 1997.

Mathews, Tom Dewe. *Censored: The Story of Film Censorship in Britain*. London: Chatto & Windus, 1994.

McCarty, John. *John McCarty's Official Splatter Movie Guide Vol. II: Hundreds More of the Grossest, Goriest, Most Outrageous Movies Ever Made!* New York: St. Martin's, 1992.

Newman, Kim. *Nightmare Movies: Horror on Screen Since the 1960s*. 2nd ed. London: Bloomsbury, 2011.

O'Neill, James. *Terror on Tape: A Complete Guide to Over 2,000 Horror Movies on Video*. New York: Billboard Books, 1995.

Rockoff, Adam. *Going to Pieces: The Rise and Fall of the Slasher Film, 1978-1986*. Jefferson, NC: McFarland, 2002.

Schoell, William. *Stay Out of the Shower: The Shocker Film Phenomenon*. London: Robinson, 1988.

Tombs, Pete. *Mondo Macabro: Weird & Wonderful Cinema Around the World*. New York: St. Martin's, 1998.

Vatnsdal, Caelum. *They Came from Within: A History of Canadian Horror Cinema*. Winnipeg, MB: Arbeiter Ring, 2004.

Weldon, Michael. *The Psychotronic Encyclopedia of Film*. London: Plexus, 1989.

MAGAZINES

Boxoffice (US; www.boxoffice.com)
DarkSide (UK; www.thedarksidemagazine.com)
Fangoria (US; www.fangoria.com)
Gorezone (US; no longer published, 1988–1993)
Gorezone (UK; no longer published, 2005–2011)
Rue Morgue (Canada; www.rue-morgue.com)
Samhain (UK; no longer published, 1986–1999)
Shivers (UK; no longer published, 1992–2008)
Starburst (UK; no longer published, 1978–2008)
Variety (US; www.variety.com)

WEBSITES

The Bodycount Continues (www.the-bodycount-continues.com)
Box Office Mojo (www.boxofficemojo.com)
Hysteria Lives! (www.hysteria-lives.co.uk)
Mobius Home Video Forum (www.mhvf.net)
Retro Slashers (www.retroslashers.net)
Slasherpool (website no longer being updated)
Smash or Trash (www.smashortrashindiefilmmaking. com)
The Terror Trap (www.terrortrap.com)
Variety (www.variety.com)

INDEX